Towards Intellectual Property Rights Management

I0011347

Dolores Modic • Nadja Damij

Towards Intellectual Property Rights Management

Back-office and Front-office Perspectives

Dolores Modic
Kyushu University
Fukuoka, Japan

Nadja Damij
Northumbria University
Newcastle upon Tyne
United Kingdom

ISBN 978-3-319-88701-2   ISBN 978-3-319-69011-7   (eBook)
https://doi.org/10.1007/978-3-319-69011-7

Cover pattern © Harvey Loake
Design of internal figures: Sara Modic

Printed on acid-free paper

This Palgrave Macmillan imprint is published by Springer Nature
The registered company is Springer International Publishing AG
The registered company address is: Gewerbestrasse 11, 6330 Cham, Switzerland

Dolores Modic • Nadja Damij

Towards Intellectual Property Rights Management

Back-office and Front-office Perspectives

Dolores Modic
Kyushu University
Fukuoka, Japan

Nadja Damij
Northumbria University
Newcastle upon Tyne
United Kingdom

ISBN 978-3-319-88701-2   ISBN 978-3-319-69011-7   (eBook)
https://doi.org/10.1007/978-3-319-69011-7

This Palgrave Macmillan imprint is published by Springer Nature
The registered company is Springer International Publishing AG
The registered company address is: Gewerbestrasse 11, 6330 Cham, Switzerland

PREFACE

Maximizing the value from innovation, in particular through intellectual property rights (IPR), is a key element of intellectual property rights (business process) management (IPRM). We take a "Robin Hood" approach, taking (learning) from the big companies to offer to smaller ones. The beauty of intangible assets is that through their use and knowledge sharing, the bigger companies are not weakened as a consequence. The adopted interdisciplinary approach provides a conceptual framework and constructs for IPR management (IPRM), derived from practical and enriched by theoretical insights. This monograph builds upon case studies and interviews with key IP executives from major multinational R&D investor firms.

The work highlights gaps in efficient IPRM, offers insights into practices used by top IP managers, and brings Tabular Application Development (TAD) methodology IPR process optimization model (using Activity Table approach) in order to highlight IPR processes and activities. The monograph provides organizational and managerial recommendations, which are especially valuable to IP(R) professionals and practitioners. Recommendations take into account both the so-called Back-office (legal and administrative) and the Front-office processes (valuing and strategizing for maximal IPR benefits to the business).

Additional features of this monograph include excerpts from interviews with some of the top IP(R) executives in the world as well as short case studies or case-in-points. What won't you find in this monograph? A magic wand that will solve all your IPR management issues. Why? Primarily because IPRM is hard. It is really hard. It is complicated for both small and big companies—from IP Rookies to top R&D investors. Do not let people tell you otherwise. What we offer here is a guide that will facilitate your journey through the jungle known as IPR.

If you are an experienced practitioner, we suggest you consult especially Chaps. 4 to 7, although the whole book is riddled with examples and recommendations that can be valuable to your everyday practice.

ACKNOWLEDGEMENTS

Dr. Modic would like to acknowledge the ARRS Grant No. ARRS-MDR-VP-2016-01/34 and the JSPS International Research Grant ID No. 16774. Dr. Damij would like to acknowledge the ARRS Grant No. ARRS-P1-0383(A).

CONTENTS

About the Authors

Dolores Modic is Japan Society for the Promotion of Science (JSPS) Fellow at Kyushu University, Japan, and 2015 Fulbright Scholar at the University of North Carolina at Chapel Hill, USA. Her research focuses on intellectual property rights and technology transfer, as well as more broadly on innovation systems and intellectual property rights management in the public and private sectors.

Nadja Damij is Senior Lecturer in Business Information Management at Newcastle Business School, Northumbria University, UK. Her research interests include business process management, specifically developing process-orientated TAD methodology. She has held a number of visiting positions at the University of Surrey, UK; University of Nevada, USA; and the Waterford Institute of Technology, Ireland.

LIST OF FIGURES

LIST OF TABLES

LIST OF BOXES

CHAPTER 1

Untangling the Intangibles: The Scope of IPR Management Research

Abstract This book provides insights into the intellectual property rights (IPR) managerial practices of key IPR executives from a range of multinational companies, including major research and development firms. It identifies gaps in IPR management and considers the Tabular Application Development (TAD) methodology IPR process optimization model. The authors adopt an interdisciplinary approach, providing a conceptual framework derived from practice and enriched with theoretical insights and offering organizational recommendations. Taking into account both Back- and Front-office processes towards intellectual property rights management will help businesses navigate the maze of IPR and maximize the value they get from innovation.

Keywords Intellectual property rights management • Back-office • Front-office • IPR experts interviews

1.1 SCOPE AND RESEARCH PROBLEM

Our book begins with the simple question, "Why bother considering intellectual property rights management issues?" Today we are living in a world riddled with intellectual property rights (IPRs) and characterized by the so-called intellectual property rights paradox. As Alkaersig et al. (2015)

© The Author(s) 2018
D. Modic, N. Damij, *Towards Intellectual Property Rights Management*, https://doi.org/10.1007/978-3-319-69011-7_1

1

have recently put it, "Large firms do it and small firms do it" (consult Box 1.1), or as Rivette and Kline (2000) wrote more than 15 years ago, "Patents aren't just for big companies anymore." Yet, especially smaller companies are still struggling with the "why's" and "how's" of intellectual property rights.[1] The paradox between the rise of IPR applications and grants on one side and IPRs' sub-optimal efficiency leads us to conclude that the management of intellectual property rights, including their processes, is of key importance to the business' success.

Box 1.1 How do the big do it? Introductory evidence from patent and trademark data of world top 2000 R&D investor firms

Patenting is a highly concentrated phenomenon; according to the OECD report World Corporate Top R&D Investors: Innovation and IP bundles (2015), the world's top 2000 R&D investors (together with their affiliates) own approximately 70% of all patent families worldwide in the five most important patent offices (European Patent Office, US Patent and Trademark Office, Korean Intellectual Property Office, Japan Patent Office, Chinese Intellectual Property Office). These IPR savvy companies differentiate their filing strategies across patent offices depending upon the technological field of the invention to protect. They rely on global knowledge to develop their technologies; hence both the invention processes of the patented technologies and the registration processes are highly international. Furthermore, patent and R&D data show that patenting is indeed an expensive endeavour with much heterogeneity across the industries. Electrical equipment companies spend in R&D on average €2M per patent family and pharmaceuticals €32M per patent family. Trademarks are mostly used for goods or related goods and services. Top R&D investors often use differentiated trademarks across markets adapting them to the consumers' expectations. The latter requires alignment between IP and marketing activities. The world of trademarks is however a more diversified one; top corporate R&D investors own on average 8% (for 2012) of all trademarks. In addition, only a few companies present technology/product combination in line with the profile of the industry in which they operate. Patents and trademarks are often bundled together and used as complementary protection mechanisms—thus displaying one side of the comprehensiveness of IPR management.

Discussions around how intangible assets, such as patents, trademarks, or design rights, are different from tangible assets are lively. However, they usually centre on the three-dimensional scope or expression of the tangibles—a fact that brings along different deliberations when dealing with one or the other, as shown in Chap. 2. But how are intellectual property rights different from other intangibles? In short, their distinctive feature is their more (not only legally) formalized nature, their geographical and temporal limitations, and the fact that they are intentionally communicated with the outside world. For example, while a trade secret loses its power once it is no longer contained inside the firm, the publication of an IPR allows for the creation of a legal foundation to employ different IPR actions. We highlight how IP(R) executives differ between tangibles and intangibles. In Chap. 5 we present how this differentiation affects the management of IP assets in practice.

Regardless of whom you ask—either an IPR Rookie or practically any of our interviewees coming from the IPR savvy world's top R&D investor firms—handling intellectual property rights is complex. IPRs are entangled in various ways. Firstly, different intellectual property rights are bundled together with each other and with other intangibles. Secondly, IPR processes are aligned with and integrated into other business processes in firms. Thirdly, different administrative, legal, and business aspects need to be taken into account, if we are to strive for efficient management of IPRs. This is a lot to consider all at once. Hence, our struggle is to try to "untangle" them in the reality permeated with uncertainty.

There seems to be a distinction between intellectual property (IP) management, innovation management, and intellectual property rights (IPR) management. Although they all centre on the management of innovation and the rights connected to them, their focus and activities differ. We will explain this first in theory and then evaluate the existence of a *sui generis* IPR management in practice. By doing so, we will consolidate the terminology used by researchers on one side and by practicing IP(R) executives on the other.

> *The overall scheme should be that we try to focus on those inventions and IP rights that are really valuable to a company. We do not need patents for themselves, we need them to add value to the company.*
>
>   *...*
>
> *In invention management you start with money and try to build ideas. On the other hand, in innovation management you try to take ideas and make*

money from them. /.../Intellectual property rights/.../are the bridge between the two. They are the bridge between having good ideas and between having inventions to creating innovations.

Chief IP Counsel,
German conglomerate manufacturing and electronics company

Some practitioners argue that IPR management deals with co-creating ideas, reducing innovations to practice, as well as making money out of them (with the emphasis on the latter). Similarly, business process management deals with business processes that are viewed as a collection of activities that take one or more kinds of input and creates an output that is of value to the customer (Brady et al. 2001) and on which firms can monetize (see Fig. 1.1).

IPR management hence means managing the so-called Back-office (legal and administrative) as well as the so-called Front-office processes, which are concerned with how IPRs can benefit the business. We emphasize that a holistic approach to efficient IPR management concerns itself in equal measures with both Back-office and Front-office. This is done by establishing a two-way link between research and legal departments on

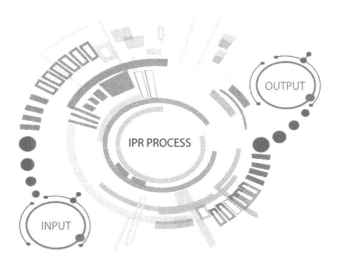

Fig. 1.1 Schematics IPR process as business process

one hand and legal, marketing, and sales departments as well as top management on the other. IPR processes should be viewed as business processes that add value and influence the performance of companies.

Business process management is essential to ensure long-term business success based on flexible, market-responsive structures that simultaneously promote efficiency (Schreer and Hoffmann 2015). This can be achieved with a powerful tacit to explicit knowledge transfer, which correlates with market changes. Such a driving force pushes innovation and its transition from intangible to tangible through the interaction Front-office—Back-office—Front-office, making a basis for efficient business process management. According to vom Brocke and Rosemann (2015), business process management can drive innovation in two ways: (1) through managing processes which yield product innovations (running processes) and (2) through managing the redesign of processes which yields process innovations (changing processes). The IPR process redesign needs to be continuous, thus based on internal change such as strategic policy change and external influences such as market, regulatory, and other forces. We not only show how some of the top R&D investor firms deal with IPR process redesign but also provide hints, for example, the usefulness of funnelling all suggestions to further IPR process (re)design backed up by the organizational structure in order to improve IPR processes.

The management of intellectual property rights (IPR management) is a vivid field. However, if we follow the opinion of some authors (e.g. Candelin-Palmquist et al. 2012), it remains underdeveloped. Issues with IPR processes are often mentioned and discussed in the literature, but they are surprisingly not so often at the core of articles, studies, or books in this field (the field of licensing being the most notable exception).

Our work is rooted in three types of works: broader knowledge management literature (with recent works such as Mohapatra et al. 2016), those dealing with business process management (such as vom Brocke and Rosemann 2015), and the literature connected to IP (or patent) management and individual IPR activities. Looking at the literature, some parts of the IPR process seem to be covered more in detail, such as legal aspects (sometimes written in a way to appeal to readers outside the legal profession) and considerations of IPR and those concerned with valuation techniques, enforcement, and patent quality (e.g. Thoma 2017; Qiao 2017; Gaesler 2016). Those however do not cover all possible aspects, elements, and activities inside the entire IPR process. Other works in general terms describe motives to patent and the way the

IPRs are used (e.g. Granstrand 2000; Cohen et al. 2000; Thumm 2001; Blind et al. 2006; Keupp et al. 2009).

The next group worth mentioning are works on the topic of so-called stage-gates (also called toll gates, milestones, etc.). They point out integration and alignment of IPR activities with R&D activities at certain points (Alkaersig et al. 2015). Next are works on the topic of patent or IPR strategy (e.g. Rimai 2016; Schmidt 2013; Jell 2012; works by Marcus Reitzig). The latter is in line with the notion that the management of IP has moved from a legal matter to a strategic issue (e.g. Gassmann and Bader 2017). Last are works dealing with IPR management, the types of organization, the involvement of staff, and the engagement of top management.

Again, although these are of key importance, they do not uncover the whole spectrum of IPR-related activities. A comprehensive overview of IPR management and process is rarely available, especially one based on insights from practice. Among the latter, single case studies tend to prevail and even those are usually quite lacking in truly offering a comprehensive overview enriched with practical recommendations. We do however suggest to the reader to immerse themselves in different approaches that however all share at least some commonalities with IPR management, such as technology roadmapping (Moehrle et al. 2013).

Although we come across the term IPR management often, there is little effort to build up theoretical constructs and operationalize them. Several frameworks and theories intersect this field, with a special emphasis on those focusing on innovation speed, agile process definition with resource allocation, as well as the efficiency of innovation. In general, IPR management occurs in a space defined by time, locality (there is supposed to be a difference between the environments of the "technology-haves" and "technology-have-nots," though these seem to differ from what traditional research has tried to depict), techno-legal scope, and technological advantage (Pitkethly 2001). This presents a complex environment for IPR management studies.

We need to keep in mind that innovation processes depend strongly on both tacit and explicit knowledge. Profiting from knowledge is the crucial aspect of intellectual property rights management. IPRs are used to create revenue, to defend the firm's competitive position, and to signal competitiveness and/or aid to engage in cooperative relationships. Hence, we can see it is not enough to create something new and potentially useful, but the emphasis is shifting towards acquiring knowledge for the appropriation of the value of innovations. Discerning how to capture value from innovation is a key element of the business model design (Teece 2010) and is the aim of process modelling. This idea permeates through IPR management, where "means have become ends" (MacDonald 2004), since IPRs have acquired a strategic value independent of the (mere) commercialization of the innovation itself.

> *One word I would use is aligned. Being integrated and aligned. What we do has to absolutely make sense with the product strategy.*
> Head of Legal Operations and IP Management,
> European multinational pharmaceutical company

To carry out business process management, it is necessary to create knowledge; this creation brings quality and effectiveness to the functioning of the organization (Damij et al. 2008). Several (knowledge) gaps can be identified in IPR management. *Inter alia*, IPR issues should be connected to other functions within the firm, such as legal, marketing, and sales. IPR management thus needs to be *ad* minimum integrated, comprehensive, and aligned, which should be incorporated into IPR process management. Several issues arise from this consequently preventing comprehensive advice for IPR management practices. We shall strive to point out the gaps and to present them in their context *via* presenting the results of interviews with IP(R) experts in the IP field.

There is a lot to consider when modelling your IPR process and IPR process flows. The Activity Table technique is a tool enabling the step-by-step trace of the flow of each process with the aim to graphically present the conversion from inputs to outputs. We use this technique with the aim of IPR process analysis, human resource allocation, and time management as well as knowledge elicitation which according to Dalkir (2005) converts tacit to explicit knowledge in order to capture it. Edvinsson and Sullivan (1996) claimed creating value in organizations from their intellectual capital is twofold: first dealing with innovations themselves and their commercialization and second dealing with the organization's business assets such as processes that "value innovation as it is converted from an intangible into a product or service for which customers will pay."

Innovation and entrepreneurship are tightly interconnected; hence, it is required that innovation be organized as a systematic activity (Drucker 2010) in the form of business processes. Throughout the last decades, the fields of business process management, and consequently business process redesign, have been gaining recognition and acceptance. The reasons for such an evolution are often cited in literature, academic publications, and research studies that deal with the theme, as well as in an increasing involvement of consultancy and software development companies (Damij et al. 2008).

Looking at IPR processes as business processes, we address specific critical points, from implementing the concept of early harvest to the clearing process step. The first allows the harvest of ideas still in an embryonic state and makes sure that IPR expertise help co-design the product or even broaden its use. The second ensures that problems due to possible further IPR clashes are avoided.

Hence, this monograph presents an overview of existing endeavours in the field of managing IPR processes. In addition, it offers an in-depth analysis of some problem areas also by using a TAD-based IPR process modelling tool. We also briefly look into the potential of so-called big data IPR analyses and try to discern the issues connected to them.

> *You can gain some insights from very big data, but I think it often breaks down on smaller data sets/.../It is always welcome that people do analyses—as long as they understand the limitations.*
>
> *Head of Legal Operations and IP Management,*
> *European multinational pharmaceutical company*

What is then the innovation potential of IPR management? In general it is well known that IPRs can be used for either offensive or defensive purposes. As for the innovation potential of IPR, some effects are easier to construct than others and can be broadly seen as contributing to the business and/or the customers. Looking at McDonalds and its franchise holder, we can easily see the benefit of the McDonald's trademark and its vigorous defence by the multinational for the franchise holder. Similar situations can be seen in most B2B relationships. Other benefits are perhaps less identifiable at first glance. Providing that the IPR process is truly both integrated and aligned, it can lead to a broader or different application or a change in the initial invention, which can render benefits for the business. For example, the contribution by the patent attorney, as one of our interviewees pointed out, can lead to broadening the scope of applicability of the invention, since an integrated procedure may bring also business and legal insights in addition to a (perhaps narrower) technical view.

One of the major problems in maximizing the value of intellectual property rights is that the link between using IPRs and the increase of the firm's profitability and the IPR use seems to be missing in many cases. Hence, IPRs may be described as probabilistic at best (Lemley and Shapiro 2005). This fact furthers our notion that the intellectual property protection processes need to be systematic, carefully designed, and thoroughly thought through (Modic and Damij 2016). Thus, it is of utmost importance that the IPR processes are designed and carried out as diligently as possible.

1.2   Aims and Methodological Approach

The approach adopted in this research venture, interdisciplinary in character, attempts to provide a conceptual framework, constructs, and offers a concrete methodology for IPR process management while combining theoretical and practical insights.

This monograph can be used as a textbook for upper undergraduate and graduate students offering developed concepts and constructs as well as business insights. By blending both the academic and industrial points of view, we provide support also to those participating in IPR processes. We aim for IPR management's increased awareness of the latest thoughts of other groups, such as academics, and vice versa. Thus, the monograph is not only meant for practitioners from the business sphere but also those who provide supporting services and supporting research (e.g. researchers in the field of IPR, BPM, providers of software tools), by providing guidelines for future research and tips on potential client needs.

The aims of this monograph are to:

1. Offer coherent constructs and conceptual frameworks for IPR management by defining IPR management as a *sui generis* subfield of business process management by:

    a. Strengthening the theoretical basis of IPR management research
    b. Defining Back-office and Front-office IPR processes and their connections

2. Highlight practices of efficient IPR management including state-of-the-art feedback from conducting interviews with IP(R) executives thereby:

    a. Investigating the difference between IP and IPR process and defining IPRM as a business process from the executives' perspective
    b. Presenting the IPR process flows by creating a generic IPRM process model

    c. Identifying knowledge (and other) gaps preventing efficient IPR management and presenting solutions to identified gaps

3. Offer an evaluation of existing IPR management models and tools for IPR process modelling giving:

    a. An in-depth analysis of a TAD methodology-based IPR modelling tool highlighting critical problems in IPR processes

We will present literature review in Chaps. 2 and 3. We will do this with the aim of helping the reader to get familiar with both key components—intellectual property rights (management) and business process management. This allows upper-level and graduate students and young researchers, as well as early stage practitioners, to comprehend the link between both areas and to better understand our focus on improvements of processes related to IPR management, as well as lessons to be learned in the following chapters. The monograph shows a process-oriented approach of IPR which is a valuable supplement to the approaches usually undertaken.

The rest of the chapters are primarily based on our research done by primary data collection through a series of interviews, with literature review offering only the backdrop for our attempt at an interdisciplinary process-oriented research. The monograph's added value lies in the presentation of the interviews, their consequent analysis, and the lessons learned allowing upper-level students to gain insights into underlying processes—something they would usually not be privy to until the beginning of their professional careers.

Special business insights and tips are offered throughout the monograph to illuminate selected issues. IP(R) practitioners (especially in smaller firms) will find useful recommendations such as taking advantage of non-costly early examination options offered by the IPR offices. Researchers or service providers can find tips such as designing optical information interfaces allowing for smoother IPR process management.

We have conducted qualitative primary data collection and analysis. This approach, especially regarding the type of interviewees and the type of collected data, is unique as the field is subject to stringent limitations connected to confidentiality and secrecy. Indeed quantitative analysis of this type is more usual; however, the data collected in that way is much more superficial. Most works are based on surveys or patent office data (usually augmented by using other sources of information). The use of interviews (apart from case studies) is rarer and usually done with less IPR savvy or smaller companies (see, e.g. the last part of Keupp et al. 2009; partially Jell

2012; Alkaersig et al. 2015). We provide the reader with an input from a niche and do this by collecting in-depth data from a variety of top-level IP executives from some of the top IPR savvy firms in the world. Furthermore, we adopt the Activity Table approach, so it can be used as an interpretative framework not only describing the IPR management activities, which is very valuable for students and researchers, but also as an easy tool to benchmark and optimize the IPR processes (for practitioners).

The monograph builds on critical literature review and first-ever published interviews' analysis and excerpts with IP(R) executives from top IPR savvy multinationals. The results will be especially of use to SMEs by illuminating not only the pitfalls and lack of efficient IPRs but also by providing insights that will help them (re)design informed processes connected to IPRs.

1.3   Chapter Summaries

The book proceeds as follows.

In Chap. 1 *Untangling the Intangibles: The Scope of IPR Management Research*, we set forth the scope and research problem of dealing with IPR management. Aims and research methods are presented together with a chapter summary.

We begin in Chap. 2 entitled *From Tangibles to Intangibles and from Back-Office to Front-Office* with the basics, as the rise of the intellectual property rights (IPR) and the general acceleration of technological advancement have caused a need for intellectual property rights fluency. First we depict if, how, and why intellectual property rights are different from other intangibles. Formal and informal IP protection mechanisms are compared in the light of business processes surrounding them. Basic IPR rights are described in short. The next section of this chapter, called En route to IPR Management: Aligning IPR Back-Office and Front-Office, is of special interest as it provides a short introduction to IPR management. Both so-called Back-office and Front-office processes connected with IPRs are taken into account.

Chapter 3 *Dealing with IPR Process Management* offers a critical overview of IPR management models to help the informative use of different IPR management tools by emphasizing their pros and cons. Inside the first part of this chapter, we look into the innovation potential of IPR management, since the inefficiency of formal IP protection mechanisms—in particular intellectual property rights—is their well-established contour.

We continue by identifying IPR processes as business processes focusing on their inputs, outputs, and activity sequencing and resource allocation that consequently enable the development of IPR process models. The modelling of IPR processes will then be evaluated through the IPR process innovation paradigm. Through the execution of above-mentioned steps, an in-depth analysis of TAD methodology as an IPR modelling approach will be presented, illuminating how it can be used for identifying critical activities, entities, paths, and bottlenecks in IPR processes. A generalized model of IPR process will be introduced as seen through the lenses of business process management paradigm. The chapter will present related definitions, constructs, and conceptual frameworks, thus aiming to strengthen the theoretical basis of IPR management.

In Chap. 4 *Interviewing IPR Executives*, we present a short methodological chapter, describing the methodology employed, especially commenting on the interviews and the connected process of data gathering and data analysis. We have divided the chapter into three parts: Who to ask and why?, How did we do it?, and Why hasn't it been done before?

Chapter 5 *IPR Management to Business Management* draws on conducted interviews and gets us one step closer to the in practice-rooted definition of IPRM. Regardless of whom you ask—either an IPR Rookie or practically any of our interviewees coming from the IPR savvy world's top R&D investor firms—handling intellectual property rights is complex. Hence, this is the first chapter that brings the analysis of interviews with IP(R) executives, including some of the world's leading multinationals.

The chapter begins with the emphasis of why they believe the IPRs are so different from other intangibles, emphasizing especially the manageability and informational value (giving thus a different focus than is usually seen in theoretical works connected to IPRs). It continues by accentuating the IP executives' views of the benefits of intellectual property rights. The reader is able to notice early on the contrast between what is put forward in the literature as the main distinction between IPR and other intangibles and what IPR executives see as their key attributes. For example, what is mostly put at the forefront by top IPR executives are the manageability and the opportunity to better control their intellectual assets as opposed to, in the literature often mentioned, temporal and geographical limitations of IPR.

We also try to get an in-depth look as to what differentiates IPR management from IP management and try to answer the questions such as whether or not we are justified to speak of IPRM in practice or in other words are IPRM and IP management one and the same thing and if this really matters. Additionally, we aim to evaluate if IPR processes are in fact business processes and consequently discover the needs companies have in connection to IPR management, combining interview results with critical literature review. Numerous plate sections containing quotes from IPR experts enrich this chapter.

In Chap. 6 *IPR Characteristics in Practice: Back-Office to Front-Office*, we answer the question of IPR management characteristics and scope. We first delve behind attributes such as "integrated," "aligned," and so on to discern what these mean in practice inside IPR savvy companies. We concern ourselves thus with what is behind these often used monikers.

The second part of this chapter looks at the strategic value of IPRM, specifically linking the strategic tasks to designing IPR strategy. Finally, the chapter tries to define the scope of IPRM through the interlude of activities defined as either Back-office, Front-office, or Mixed, thus extending on the last part of Chap. 5. This part shows not only the complementarity of legal and administrative tasks with business-oriented tasks but also the extensive inclusion of different employees and different departments as is not only seen in presented flowcharts of IPR process activities but also in property tables. The chapter is enriched with various citations by the top IP executives. We also give some interview-based recommendation for successful IPR Back-office and Front-office practices.

Chapter 7 *IPR Management in Action: The Road to "Better" IPR Management* expands upon the previous chapters especially on empirical data gathered in Chaps. 5 and 6 from the interviews. In this chapter we first point out the human resource dimension of IPRM and then deal with the elementary question of whether or not formalization brings optimization. Not surprisingly, due to the type of respondents, the prevailing attitude is that of agreeing with the premise of formalization bringing opportunities for optimization. We briefly show what top IP executives have in mind when saying so. Based on the identified inefficiencies, and using the TAD IPR model, as the interpretative framework describing the IPR management practices more in depth, we first also consider what you should worry about when designing or re-modelling your IPR processes.

The rest of the chapter delivers the IPR Activity Table—bringing the activities and the connected administrative, legal, and especially business considerations. Using the TAD IPR model, we are able to introduce to the reader the practice of the tabular method presenting the links between the identified IPR-related activities and people involved in them. Additionally, the model's analysis points out the possible gaps as well as the more appropriate people to carry out the activities.

The chapter introduces signposts leading to increasing efficiency of intellectual property rights process management in companies. Although all chapters contain recommendations, they are especially valuable inside this chapter as they are tightly connected to the gaps within the intellectual property rights processes. We warmly suggest this chapter to all practitioners as well as all students and researchers interested in the practical intricacies of the processes connected to IPRs.

Chapter 8 *Conclusion: Optimizing IPR Processes* presents the conclusion of the research emphasizing the main conclusions and presenting directions on how to untangle the intangibles and thereby optimize IPR processes.

NOTES

1. Some works thus focus in particular on start-ups (especially those knowledge intensive start-ups, due to the fact that their IPR is their main asset and thus IP needs need to be considered early and extensively (McManus 2012; Halt et al. 2017)).

REFERENCES

Alkaersig, L., Beukel, K., & Reichstein, T. (2015). *Intellectual property rights management: Rookies, dealers and strategists*. Hampshire: Palgrave.

Blind, K., Edler, J., Frietsch, R., & Schmoch, U. (2006). Motives to patent: Evidence from Germany. *Research Policy, 35*, 655–672.

Brady, A. J., et al. (2001). *Concepts in enterprise resource planning*. Boston: Course Technology Thomson Learning.

Candelin-Palmquist, H., Sanberg, B., & Mylly, U. M. (2012). Intellectual property rights in innovation management research: A review. *Technovation, 32*(2012), 502–512.

Cohen, W. M., Nelson, R. R., & Walsh, J. P. (2000). *Protecting their intellectual assets: Appropriability conditions and why U.S. manufacturing firms patent (or not)*. Cambridge, MA: NBER.

Dalkir, K. (2005). *Knowledge management in theory and practice*. Amsterdam: Elsevier Butterworth-Heinmann.

Damij, N., Damij, T., Grad, J., & Jelenc, F. (2008). A methodology for business process improvement and IS development. *Information and Software Technology, 50*(2008), 1127–1141.

Drucker, P. F. (2010). *Innovation and entrepreneurship*. Oxford and Burlington: Elsevier.

Edvinsson, L., & Sullivan, P. (1996). Developing a model for managing intellectual capital. *European Management Journal, 14*(4), 356–364.

Gaesler, F. (2016). *Enforcing and trading patents: Evidence for Europe*. Wiesbaden: Springer Fachmedien.

Gassmann, O., & Bader, M. A. (2017). *Patentmanagement: Innovationen erfolgreich nutzen und schützen*. Berlin and Heidelberg: Springer.

Granstrand, O. (2000). Corporate innovation systems. A comparative study of multi-technology corporations in Japan, Sweden and the USA. Paper submitted to the Dynacom project. Retrieved from http://www.lem.sssup.it/Dynacom/D21.html

Halt, G. B., Donch, J. C., Stiles, A. R., & Fesnak, R. (2017). *Intellectual property and financing strategies for technology startups*. Cham: Springer Science and Business Media.

Jell, F. (2012). Patent filling strategies and patent management: An empirical study. Gabler Verlag and Springer Fachmedien, Wiesbaden.

Keupp, M. M., Beckenbauer, A., & Gassmann, O. (2009). How managers protect intellectual property rights in China using de facto strategies. *R&D Management, 39*(2), 211–224.

Lemley, M. A., & Shapiro, C. (2005). Probabilistic patents. *Journal of Economic Perspectives, 19*(2), 75–98.

Macdonald, S. (2004). When means become ends: Considering the impact of patent strategy on innovation. *Information Economics and Policy, 16*(1), 135–158.

McManus, J. P. (2012). *Intellectual property: From creation to commercialisation: A practical guide for innovators & researchers*. Cork: Oak Tree Press.

Modic, D., & Damij, N. (2016). "Own-it": Managing intellectual property processes via the activity table in creative industries. In A. Lugmayr, E. Stojmenova, K. Stanoevska, & R. Wellington (Eds.), *Information systems and management in eMedia and entertainment*. Heidelberg, New York, Dordrecht and London: Springer.

Moehrle, M. G., Isenmann, R., & Phaal, R. (Eds.). (2013). *Technology roadmapping for strategy and innovation: Charting the route to success*. Heidelberg, New York, Dordrecht and London: Springer.

Mohapatra, S., Agrawal, A., & Satpathy, A. (2016). *Designing knowledge management-enabled business strategies: A top-down approach*. Heidelberg, New York, Dordrecht and London: Springer.

OECD. (2015). *OECD world corporate top R&D investors: Innovation and IP bundles*. Paris: OECD.

Pitkethly, R. H. (2001). Intellectual property strategy in Japanese and UK companies: Patent licensing decisions and learning opportunities. *Research Policy, 30*(2001), 425–442.

Qiao, Y. (Ed.). (2017). *Maintenance time and the industry development of patents: Empirical research with evidence from China*. Singapore: Springer Science+Business Media Singapore.

Rimai, D.S. (2016). Patent engineering: A guide to building a valuable patent portfolio and controlling the marketplace. Scrivener Publishing and Wiley, Hoboken, NJ.

Rivette, K. G., & Kline, D. (2000). *Rembrandts in the attic: Unlocking the hidden value of patents*. Boston: Harvard Business School Press.

Schmidt, M. P. (2013). Patent strategies in the process-related industries: Outline of the problems. *R&D Management, 43*(3), 242–251.

Schreer, A. W., & Hoffmann, M. (2015). The process of business process management. In J. vom Brocke & M. Rosemann (Eds.), *Handbook on business process management 2. Strategic alignment, governance, people and culture. International handbooks on information systems* (2nd ed., pp. 101–132). Heidelberg, New York, Dordrecht and London: Springer.

Teece, D. (2010). Business models, business strategy and innovation. *Long Range Planning, 43*(2010), 172–194.

Thoma, G. (2017). *Patent management and valuation: The strategic and geographical dimension*. New York: Routledge.

Thumm, N. (2001). Management of intellectual property rights in European biotechnology firms. *Technological Forecasting and Social Change, 67*, 259–272.

vom Brocke, J., & Rosemann, M. (Eds.). (2015). *Handbook on business process management 2. Strategic alignment, governance, people and culture. International handbooks on information systems* (2nd ed. pp. 101–132). Heidelberg, New York, Dordrecht and London: Springer.

CHAPTER 2

From Tangibles to Intangibles and from Back-Office to Front-Office

Abstract The rise of the intellectual property rights and the general acceleration of technological advancement have caused a need for IP fluency. We begin with the basics in this chapter. First we depict if, how, and why intellectual property rights are different from other intangibles. Formal and informal IP protection mechanisms are compared in the light of business processes surrounding them. Basic IPR are described in short. The next section provides a short introduction on IPR management. Both so-called Back-office and Front-office processes connected with IPRs are taken into account.

Keywords Intangibles • Intellectual property rights • Back-office • Front-office

2.1 WHY ARE INTELLECTUAL PROPERTY RIGHTS DIFFERENT TO OTHER INTANGIBLES?

Clearly intangible goods (or assets), such as patents, trademarks, or designs, are different from tangible goods in numerous ways. While tangible goods have a three-dimensional scope or expression, intangibles do

D. Modic, N. Damij, *Towards Intellectual Property Rights Management*, https://doi.org/10.1007/978-3-319-69011-7_2

not (or at least need not have them). This presents a problem when they need to be protected from third parties, due to the difficulties in their protection. Furthermore, business people often have difficulties in assessing the value of intangibles.

The mechanisms for intellectual property protection may be distinguished between formal (patents, models, designs, trademarks, etc.) and informal mechanisms (trade secrets, first on the market, complementary goods, etc.) (Hall et al. 2014; Neuheusler 2009; Rammer 2002). The array of IP mechanisms is wide. We sometimes speak of registered or statutory protected IP mechanisms and those that are not. Intellectual property rights doubtlessly belong to the first group (for some others, such as trade secrets, this classification is not always so straightforward). Nonetheless, the attitudes of business people—especially inside smaller companies—towards intellectual property rights are many times more in terms of regarding them as a nuisance than a useful tool to protect the intangibles.

How are intellectual property rights different from other intangibles? Firstly, their distinctive feature is their more formalized nature. They demand codified knowledge in order to be able to exist. There are many variations of activities connected to transferring tacit knowledge to explicit—the best are those allowing for early invention spotting. Secondly, they have distinct geographical and temporal limitations, for example, a patent will be valid in a certain territory for a certain amount of time. Beyond that it has no direct legal consequences. The business strategy must incorporate that fact *ex ante* to compensate for any possible negative effects. Thirdly, they are intentionally communicated with the outside. While a trade secret loses its power once it is no longer contained inside the firm, the publication of an IPR allows for the creation of the legal foundation to employ different IPR actions. Fourthly, managing knowledge incorporated in a patent that is open to the outside (due to IPRs being published) requires the development of specific IPR strategies and their underlying activities, distinct of those when dealing with informal IP protection mechanisms.

Before moving on, let us dedicate a couple of words to each of the major types of (formal) intellectual property rights (IPRs).

The expression "patent" is based on the Latin "litterae patentis" or "open letters," which were issued by sovereigns and meant for whoever the gift or benefit was intended. Today a patent provides patent owners the right to exclude others for a limited time (usually 20 years) from using an invention (technical invention, or in some legal regimes software and/or business methods). The boundaries of the invention protection are delineated by the so-called claims in a granted patent document, where the holder of the patent has disclosed important information about the invention. Although it is often asserted that a patent is a property right given monopoly and "like any property right, its boundaries should be clear" (see, e. g. a US court case from 2002 Festo Corp. v. Shoketsu Kinzoku Kogyo 2002), this is often not so.

The patent is based on three (more or less universal) criteria: novelty, non-obviousness, and industrial capability (with the latter being the fuzziest one in practice). The inventions need to be new and previously not disclosed (a requirement IP Rookies sometimes fail to observe) as well as need to have an inventive step to be patentable.

Patents are in their essence negative rights. They are often described as monopolies, but in a sense of a legal monopoly and not necessarily of an economic one. Patent protection is many times porous, imperfect, and uncertain. Nonetheless, firms can skilfully enhance the impact of patent rights through coordinated, integrated, and aligned actions related to obtaining, maintaining, using, or enforcing patents, although these processes are typically resource intensive (Somaya 2012).

Patents can be used for product enhancement (implementing the solution in a service or good sold directly on the goods market) to protect an advantage in the production process (although for such inventions individuals need to think deeply about whether a trade secret mechanism is not more appropriate), ensuring freedom to operate, selling or licensing (thus generating revenues on the so-called market for ideas—i.e. out-licensing), utilizing them as a guarantee or a financial asset, or using them to build cooperation with other firms or simply as a bargaining chip, creating power over suppliers (Reitzig (2004) gives a nice example of this by Nokia), putting them in a patenting pool, or simply donating them (for various reasons that are sometimes connected to business strategic decisions, sometimes to philanthropic activities by the firms). The desired output of a patent IPR process can vary in accordance with the overall strategic IPR goals of the company and their operationalization inside an individual IPR process, from profiting from them directly (e.g. via licensing fees) to establishing a new IPR-based cooperation and so on. Once the protection ends, the patent reverses to public good, although with various strategies firms can try to influence that that certain type of solution will remain closed off to its rivals (e.g. by creating patent fences).

A *trademark* allows for the distinction of goods or services of a certain firm from others. Their primary purpose is derived from attempts to regulate the competitive relationships between firms (Cornish et al. 2010; Bently and Sherman 2009). They are as such a part of firms' "goodwill." Some believe trademarks are as old as trade itself. Their functions were upgraded during history: from simple indications of who made a certain good to the function of quality guarantee to finance and marketing. The latter also means that other parts of the company (beyond IP(R) or legal departments) are more susceptible to their importance. They are also faster, cheaper, and usually easier to obtain.

As much as we cannot speak of registered and non-registered patents (in so far as we do not simply call them trade secrets), we do distinguish both registered and non-registered trademarks. Both protect a specific brand or an image. However, despite the fact that trademarks are governed by the principle of "use-it-or-lose-it" and some countries employ the first-to-use regulation, a lot of companies will choose to register their trademark(s). They are also far cheaper to register (and maintain) than patents. This mirrors itself in the fact that trademarks are the most voluminous IPR. Today a trademark provides its owner an exclusive right (trademark in its essence is also a negative right) to prevent others from marketing the same or similar trademarks (which is generally a word, phrase, symbol, or design (including 3D shapes), or more exotic ones such as scent or a combination thereof). A mark needs to be distinctive— that is, it must be capable of identifying the source of a particular good or service (in some jurisdictions also the term "service mark" is used; however, it follows the regulations as put down for trademarks). The rights to a trademark can be lost through abandonment, a lack of paying the registration fee, improper licensing or assignment, or genericity (consider the case below in Box 2.1).

Box 2.1 Did you ever consider what elevator, zipper, yo-yo, cellophane, and aspirin have in common?
They all started as trademarks, but then began being used as generalized terms—hence, the companies owning them lost their trademark (either just in some countries—e.g. yo-yo still enjoys protection in Canada but is not protected in the USA for the past 40 years—or overall). This is sometimes called "genericide" (or genericization). It describes the process of a former brand name or trademark becoming generic and thus losing its legal protection. In other words, marks, which were once distinctive, have over time become descriptive or used to generally define a class of goods—and thus no longer serve to identify the goods of a particular manufacturer, losing one of the key attributes, distinctiveness. Getting worldwide recognition of your mark can thus be a double-edged sword. For this not to happen, companies must realize this could indeed happen to them and hence they might lose a very valuable trademark. For example, Twitter raised concerns about brand genericide in its initial public offering (2013), writing: "There is a risk that the word 'Tweet' could become so commonly used that it becomes synonymous with any short comment posted publicly on the internet, and if this happens, we could lose protection of this trademark." This concern is of a more general nature, but already recognizes a potential problem and can lead to a strategic positioning against this occurrence (we address IP strategies theoretically in the next subchapter and point out some critical points as seen by our interviewees in Chap. 6). To go beyond this, a cooperation with IP departments, marketing departments, and sometimes others is necessary (we start Chap. 7 by emphasizing the HR dimension of intellectual property rights management). This is how some companies have started campaigns, such as the case of Xerox with "When you use 'Xerox' the way you use 'Aspirin', we get a headache" or the company Rollerblade, with their ad "Incorrect: Eating raw poultry, marrying your sibling, 'rollerblading'." The latter serving to remind us to use in-line skating as the generic term, or flying disk instead of Frisbee or even using air bubble cushioning material instead of Bubble Wrap. And yes, not to "google." All in all, trademarks are extremely valuable, for example, Google trademark is valued at tens of billions of US dollars—and if

the task of IPRM and business as a whole is to exploit their intangibles as much as they can, generalization is to be feared from an IPR point of view.

Sources:

Twitter. (2013). Initial public offering of shares of common stock of Twitter, Inc. Retrieved from https://www.sec.gov/Archives/edgar/data/1418091/000119312513390321/d564001ds1.htm#toc564001_4

WIPO Magazine. (2009). What you don't know about trademarks. Retrieved from http://www.wipo.int/wipo_magazine/en/2009/06/article_0010.html#1

WIPR Magazine. (2016). Xerox: Avoiding a 'genericide' headache. Retrieved from http://www.worldipreview.com/article/xerox-avoiding-a-genericide-headache

Garber, M. (2014). 'Kleenex is a registered trademark' (and other desperate appeals). *The Atlantic*, September 25, 2014. Retrieved from https://www.theatlantic.com/business/archive/2014/09/kleenex-is-a-registered-trademark-and-other-appeals-to-journalists/380733/

Tulett, S. (2014). 'Genericide': Brands destroyed by their own success. *BBC News*, May 28, 2014. Retrieved from http://www.bbc.com/news/business-27026704

Greenberg, J. (2017). The pitfall of trademark genericide: When household names and brands collide. Retrieved from https://masur.com/lawtalk/trademark-genericide/

Designs or design rights could also be called the "poor relative" inside the IPR family. In the last few years, somewhat more emphasis is given to them. This is due to the growth of general interest in IPRs, as well as reports of high paid damages for infringement, the claimed inadequacy of judicial decisions, and some discussions on the availability and usability of these protection mechanisms for certain types of products—such as fashion apparel.

Design rights are exclusive rights to the visual appearance (either of a product as a whole or a part of the product—have you ever notice the little shapes and lines in paper towels? Yes, they are most probably protected by design rights). The appearance needs to be original and sufficiently different from others. However, the design right is usually in practice narrow; hence, the idea is to keep the competitors from directly copying your product and not so much in preventing similar products to enter the market. Designs can, similarly to trademarks, also exist as non-registered designs. The decision on which route to take is usually a business decision—note that registered designs are usually cheaper and faster to get than patents; on the other hand, the legal scope of the right is rather limited.

The very beginnings of *copyrights* are related to censorship and publishing guilds in the sixteenth century. So the beginnings had more to do with state control or control of a certain interest group; however, by the late seventeenth century or beginning of the eighteenth century, the history of the modern copyrights began (Cornish et al. 2010; Bently and Sherman 2009). A copyright is a typical *droit d'author*, meaning it does not need registering in the majority of systems, but is obtained automatically with the creation and articulation. It is used heavily in the creative industries and mostly lasts either 50 years or 70 years after the author's death. *Copyrights* usually protect literary, musical, dramatic, choreographic, pictorial or graphic, audiovisual, or architectural works, or sound recordings, from being reproduced without the permission of the copyright owner. Interestingly in the EU, this is also the (only officially available) protection mechanism for software in itself,[1,2] which has according to some kept it in the forefront of business-related IPR.

Trade secrets and copyrights are similar in terms that there is no official registration procedure (although historically this does not hold for copyrights as some options to externally announce them were (and are) available). Trade secrets are non-formal mechanisms for protecting the IP (with the most popular one being the first-to-market mechanism according to some research—although disputed by others, e.g. Boutellier and Heinzen (2014) speak about the myth of the Pioneer); nonetheless, some level of formality is needed, so their enforcement could be efficient (e.g. labelling it as a trade secret by indicating this is a piece of information specific to the firm and with the quality of obtaining some economic advantage; taking measures to keep this information non-obtainable to the outside). Nonetheless, the sub-process of IPR registration—together with its different considerations—is not needed here. This also causes a lower financial strain on the company and demands somewhat less IPR-related knowledge and skills. On the other hand, when commercializing them via licensing, this can be a complicated task (consult also the first section of Chap. 5 for more on this). Various jurisdictions grant different kinds of information on legal protection. In terms of invention, it is well established that for some inventions, trade secrets are a preferable protection mechanisms (e.g. for process inventions).

The term used often in relation to the above-mentioned IPRs is also "assets" in order to be recognized by the business managers and IP executives that intellectual property rights are not only legal rights but also present (at least potential) economic benefits. In other words, we can speak of intangibles as assets as soon as we consider knowledge embodied in them as a form of property capable of bringing a commercial benefit. IPRs also ensure economic value to human talent, since talent (skills, experiences, etc.) is in its nature non-proprietary and does not have a legal status (excluding that that is bind to the employer-employee relationship that goes beyond IPRs (WIPO 2016)—in line with what Dodgson et al. (2014) point out, that, broadly defined, a company's reputation, mindset, and culture for innovation can also be seen as intangible assets). It is the people (or the human capital) that create and manage the IPRs, and their decisions will determine their ultimate business effects.

The selection of a specific mechanism is crucial for all subsequent processes related to the protection of the intellectual property. Some believe that a dual approach, which comprises of combining formal and informal mechanisms, is the most effective (Kitching and Blackburn 2007; Cohen et al. 2000; Levin et al. 1987). However, when looking at intellectual property rights, also its subsequent management plays a vital role—such as deciding on the *mode d'emploi* of intellectual property rights. The opening line of the book *Licensing Intellectual Property: Law & Management* by Raman Mittal says something similar: "Profitably monetizing [intellectual property] is usually harder than getting it in the first place."

There are many works emphasizing the importance of the "right time" in innovation or IPR processes. Nonetheless, right time does not always mean "the need for speed," as is the case, for example, with the strategy of first on the market (as a non-formal mechanism of invention protection and a mode allowing for at least short-term appropriation of value derived from a big market share). But let us remind ourselves of the idea behind the patent system: limited time monopoly in exchange for the publication of the invention inside the patent document. From the point of view of the patentee, the first is highly desirable, the second a nuisance. Because of that they try to optimize the time point in which the rest of the world will be able to see the content of their patent. This can mean trying to prolong this time, or in some instances to shorten this time. Did you know that in his work, Jell (2012) discovered that more than 50% of all filings involve applicant-induced delays in patent registration processes, when looking at German patent office data.

Managing intellectual property rights or IPR management is hence complex and to a point needs to be complex. What do we mean by saying "it needs to be complex"? Intellectual property rights processes need codified knowledge and are very dependent on the regulatory environment, and in order for the IPR management to be able to perform its informative function, it requires complexity. The latter can be derived from various inputs that are needed in the IPR process.

2.2   En Route to IPR Management: Aligning IPR Back-Office and Front-Office

There is a plethora of expressions dominating the field of innovation management in general. These complementaries, often integrated and aligned mutually reinforcing disciplines (such as innovation management, technology management or R&D management, intellectual property management, and intellectual property rights management), help companies capture the value from innovation. Among them innovation management seems to be the original phenotype and intellectual property rights management—with some of its distinct characteristics—its genotype or hyponym.

While looking into the issue of intellectual property rights management (IPRM), we need to take into account that companies encounter the problem of the low effectiveness of all mechanisms for protecting their intellectual property in general (see, e. g. Cohen et al. 2000; Levin et al. 1987). However, we must point out that some authors claim that the effects of intellectual property rights may be today seen more in terms of playing the role of innovation barriers in terms of competition than as an innovation enablers (see, e.g. WIPO 2011; Boldrin and Levine 2008; MacDonald 2004). Furthermore, usual criticism is directed towards their costliness, low effectiveness, and delays related to their acquisition (Blackburn 2007; Cohen et al. 2000; Levin et al. 1987). Companies often also do not possess sufficient knowledge to use IPRs as efficiently as possible. This is especially true for smaller- and medium-sized (SME) companies (Holgersson 2013; Lanjouw and Schankerman 2004; Blackburn 2007). The informality of SMEs' business processes often does not seem to be conductive of successful IP(R) processes.

Already in the 1990s, and the beginning of the 2000s, surveys of the Fortune 100 or Fortune 500 companies estimated that much of their wealth comes from their IPRs; for example, a 2002 research stated that 45% to 75% of Fortune 500 companies' wealth comes from their IPRs (Cockburn 2015). Reitzig (2004) thus notes that in such an environment of capital-intensive IPRs with long-term business effects, "IP management cannot be left to technology managers or corporate legal staff alone." These individuals are skilled in generating inventions and legal-administrative tasks; however, the so-called Front-office IPR tasks are often beyond their expertise, and hence managing IPRs needs to be of concern also to business unit leaders as well as top-level executives.

Managing intellectual property rights will thus have at least two dimensions on the level of individual processes: one is the legal-administrative dimension, the other a business dimension (combined with later mentioned strategic dimension). Hence, IPR management means managing the so-called Back-office side of it (legal and administrative) as well as the so-called Front-office processes. The latter are concerned with how IPRs can benefit the business (and is highly connected to the strategic dimension). These two expressions were also used recently by the CPA (2014) report and are mostly recognized by the IP executives.

> *Both are important. You need to manage the Back-Office in the best possible way, because there you create the assets—and they need to be of quality. On the other hand, you need to exploit and extract value [Front-Office].*
> *Chief Intellectual Property Officer,*
> *European telecommunications company*

To ensure long-term business success based on flexible, market-responsive structures that simultaneously promote efficiency (Schreer and Hoffmann 2015), a powerful tacit to explicit knowledge transfer, in strong correlation with market changes, is needed. Such a driving force is pressuring innovation and its transition from intangible to tangible through the interaction Front-office—Back-office—Front-office. Several dimensions need to be mentioned.

Firstly, *time* is one of the elements that is extremely relevant. In the literature on innovation, the elapsed time between the initial discovery and its commercialization is defined as innovation speed (Kessler and Chakrabarti 1996; Markman et al. 2005). Sonnenberg (1993) notes that innovation speed is a capability which can yield significant competitive advantage when combined with core processes. Innovation speed theory is thus inextricably related to time, where time is seen as a scarce resource due to inherent depreciation of the value of innovations. Research on innovation speed has been grounded in two theoretical streams, economics and management. Inside the first the researchers were mainly concerned with the innovation speed capturing the rate at which innovation is diffused throughout populations of organizations, regions, and nations. Inside the second innovation speed refers to the rate at which discoveries are converted into rent-producing assets (Eisenhardt and Martin 2000; Kessler and Chakrabarti 1996; Markman et al. 2005). But inside IPR processes, both the initial point in time and the final point in time are relevant. Managing time inside IPR processes is among one of the key skills needed—it is usually not about being fast, or being slow, but about being "on time," as was recently reiterated by members of the industry at the OECD STI Micro-lab event (2016). Inside this "time game" the interaction between the so-called Front-office and Back-office is vital.

Secondly, we have the issue of the *organizational infrastructure*. Some speak of the Intellectual Property Management System (e.g. Karuna and Vandana 2006). According to *ibid*. it is a managerial tool that helps accumulate and further ensures the value of the IP portfolio. In an organizational sense, such a system encompasses a set of rules, formalized processes, developed best practices as well as (software) IP(R) management tools. The IPR Back-office will traditionally be one of the most formalized parts of an organization, due to external pushes (e.g. legislative demands) as well as internal pulls (e.g. the strive to ensure optimal information function of the IPR management). Furthermore, the Back-office needs to be aligned with the needs of the Front-office, so it can provide the needed data (in the desired timeframe). Next, the Front-office needs to be tightly interconnected with both the management team and other parts of the firm (such as marketing). The Back-office helps IPR management in the service of inventors and creators; the Front-office on the other hand needs to be set up and integrated in a way which ensures capturing maximum value from IPRs to benefit the business as a whole.

Thirdly, the role of *human capital* is of key importance. Both IP professionals completing the tasks of the Front-office (FO) as well as Back-office (BO) need to be taken into account, if we are to truly talk about managing IPR processes (see Fig. 2.1). The tasks of IP professionals and others involved in IPR process and activities are various, for example: draft claims for inventors (BO); advise inventors and creators (BO/FO); determine geographical

Fig. 2.1 The interplay of Back-office and Front-office

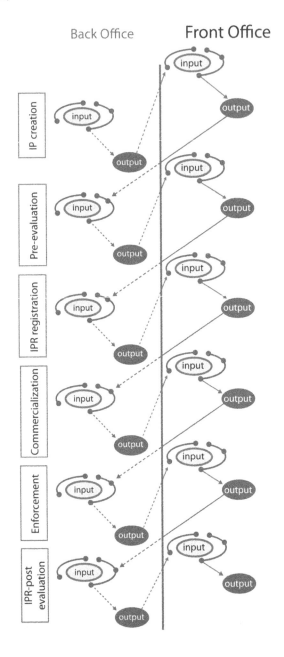

scope when registering IP rights (BO/FO); help develop business IP strategies (FO); negotiate IP licensing, joint venture agreements, advise on joining patent pools, and so on (FO); provide counsel on IP valuation (BO/FO); manage IP portfolios (BO/FO); engage in activities related to the protection of the IP (FO/BO); and so on. The combination of IPRs and human capital is a potent business force. However, in order for this to be true, the Back-office and Front-office activities need to be aligned and integrated not only with each other but also with other business activities. Special attention needs to be given to smooth and interconnected flows of activities, where the outputs of one activity translate to inputs into the next activity.

We have argued before for the so-called "own-it" principle (Modic and Damij 2016). Only quality IP creation (not having in mind the original "spark," but rather the continuation of the path to the stage of exploitation) and good IPR management may provide a sufficient basis for the successful exploitation of intellectual property rights that are entangled in various ways. Different intellectual property rights are bundled together with each other and with other intangibles; IPR processes are aligned with and integrated into business processes in firms; in addition different administrative, legal, and business aspects need to be taken into account if we are to strive for the efficient management of IPRs. Thus, today firms are in serious need of "untangling the intangibles" in order to be able to harvest the full potential of IPR management.

NOTES

1. Under the EPC, a computer program claimed "as such" is not a patentable invention (Article 52(2)(c) and (3) EPC). Patents are not granted for program listings alone, which are protected by copyrights. For a patent to be granted for a computer-implemented invention, a technical problem has to be solved in a novel and nonobvious manner. Thus, it is sometimes up to having (or locating) sufficient know-how to be able to register them as patents and not rely on less comprehensive copyright.
2. We could also divide it in another way (following Pitkethly 2001): the internal management of IPR (with the tasks of running the IP department itself and managing the interactions with other departments inside the company) and the external management of IPRs, concerned primarily with how firms interact with third party IPRs. Nonetheless, we find the selected taxonometry more telling as both Front- and Back-office can be concerned with both internal management and so-called external management inside particular activities.

References

Blackburn, R. A. (Ed.). (2007). *Intellectual property and innovation management in small firms.* London and New York: Routledge.

Bently, L., & Sherman, B. (2009). *Intellectual property law* (3rd ed.). Oxford: Oxford University Press.

Boldrin, M., & Levine, D. K. (2008). *Against intellectual monopoly.* Cambridge and New York: Cambridge University Press.

Boutellier, R., & Heinzen, M. (2014). *Growth through innovation: Managing the technology-driven enterprise.* Cham, Heidelberg, New York, Dordrecht and London: Springer.

Cockburn, I. (2015). Assessing the value of a patent: Things to bear in mind. Retrieved from http://www.wipo.int/sme/en/documents/valuing_patents_fulltext.html#P3_81

Cohen, W. M., Nelson, R. R., & Walsh, J. P. (2000). *Protecting their intellectual assets: Appropriability conditions and why U.S. manufacturing firms patent (or not).* Cambridge, MA: NBER.

Cornish, W., Llewelyn, D., & Aplin, T. (2010). *Intellectual property: Patents, copyright, trade marks and allied rights* (7th ed.). London: Sweet and Maxwell.

CPA. (2014). Driving IP value. Better investments, increasing returns. *White Paper.* Retrieved from http://www.cpaglobal.com/wp-content/uploads/2016/06/Driving-IP-Value-Whitepaper-Final.pdf

Dodgson, M., Gann, D. M., & Phillips, N. (2014). Perspectives on innovation management. In M. Dodgson, D. M. Gann, & N. Phillips (Eds.), *The Oxford handbook of innovation management.* Oxford: Oxford University Press.

Eisenhardt, K. M., & Martin, J. A. (2000). Dynamic capabilities: What are they? *Strategic Management Journal, 21,* 1105–1121.

Festo Corp. v. Shoketsu Kinzoku Kogyo Kabushiki Co. (2002), 535 U.S. 722.

Hall, B., Helmers, C., Rogers, M., & Sena, V. (2014). The choice between formal and informal intellectual property: A review. *Journal of Economic Literature, 52*(2), 1–50.

Holgersson, M. (2013). Patent management in entrepreneurial SMEs: A literature review and an empirical study of innovation appropriation, patent propensity, and motives. *R&D Management, 43*(1), 21–36.

Jell, F. (2012). *Patent filling strategies and patent management: An empirical study.* Wiesbaden: Gabler Verlag; Springer Fachmedien.

Karuna, J., & Vandana, S. (2006). Intellectual property management system: An organizational perspective. *Journal of Intellectual Property Rights, 11*(2006), 330–333.

Kessler, E. H., & Chakrabarti, A. K. (1996). Innovation speed: A conceptual model of context, antecedents, and outcomes. *The Academy of Management Review, 21*(4), 1143–1191.

Kitching, J., & Blackburn, R. A. (2007). Innovation, intellectual property and informality: Evidence from a study of small enterprises and some implications for policy. In R. A. Blackburn (Ed.), *Intellectual property and innovation management in small firms* (pp. 16–34). London and New York: Routledge.

Lanjouw, J. O., & Schankerman, M. (2004). Protecting intellectual property rights: Are small firms handicapped? *Journal of Law and Economics, 47*(1), 45–74.

Levin, R. C., Klevorick, A. K., Nelson, R. R., & Winter, S. G. (1987). Appropriating the returns from industrial research and development. *Brookings Papers on Economic Activity, 1987*(3), 783–831.

Macdonald, S. (2004). When means become ends: Considering the impact of patent strategy on innovation. *Information Economics and Policy, 16*(1), 135–158.

Markman, G. D., Gianiodis, P. T., Phan, P., & Balkin, D. B. (2005). Innovation speed: Transferring university technology to market. *Research Policy, 34*, 1058–1075.

Modic, D., & Damij, N. (2016). "Own-it": Managing intellectual property processes via the activity table in creative industries. In S. Lugmayr & W. Stanoevska (Eds.), *Information systems and management in eMedia industry* (pp. 101–117). Cham: Springer.

Neuheusler, P. (2009). *Formal vs. informal protection instruments and the strategic use of patents in an Expected-Utility framework*. Fraunhofer ISI Discussion Papers Innovation Systems and Policy Analysis, No. 20, Fraunhofer ISI, Karlsruhe.

OECD STI Micro-lab event. (2016). Microdata-lab meets Industry First users' day, June 28, 2016, Wien.

Pitkethly, R. H. (2001). Intellectual property strategy in Japanese and UK companies: Patent licensing decisions and learning opportunities. *Research Policy, 30*(2001), 425–442.

Rammer, C. (2002). *Patente und Marken als Schutzmechanismen für Innovationen*. Studien zum deutschen Innovationssystem, Nr. 11-2003, Zentrum für Europäische Wirtschaftsforschung (ZEW), Mannheim.

Reitzig, M. (2004). Strategic management of intellectual property. *MIT Sloan Management Revue, 45*(3), 35–40.

Schreer, A. W., & Hoffmann, M. (2015). The process of business process management. In J. vom Brocke & M. Rosemann (Eds.), *Handbook on business process management 2: Strategic alignment, governance, people and culture* (pp. 351–380).

Somaya, D. (2012). Patent strategy and management: An integrative review and research agenda. *Journal of Management, 38*(4), 1084–1114.

Sonnenberg, H. (1993). Balancing speed and quality in product innovation. *Canadian Business Review, 17*(3), 19–22.

WIPO. (2011). *World intellectual property report 2011: The changing face of innovation*. Geneva: WIPO.

WIPO. (2016). *IP asset development and management: A key strategy for economic growth*. IP Assets Management Series. Geneva: WIPO. Retrieved from http://www.wipo.int/edocs/pubdocs/en/intproperty/896/wipo_pub_896.pdf

CHAPTER 3

Innovation Property Rights Process Management

Abstract We start by identifying IPR processes as business processes focusing on their inputs, outputs, and activity sequencing and resource allocation that consequently enable the development of IPR process models. Additionally, we look at various business process definitions in order to set foundations for the empirical research in the following chapters.

The modelling of IPR processes will then be presented by the use of the TAD modelling approach and the steps necessary to transform the IPRM process into a business process model. Both business process modelling and the Activity Table technique are used to identify the value-added IPRM process outputs and, if necessary, refocus the IPR process to achieve this.

Keywords Business asset • IPR strategy • Business process management • Activity Table • TAD methodology

3.1   Untangling Innovation Potential via IPR Management

Studying IPR management is important due to the differing abilities of companies and other organizations to obtain benefits from innovation as well as IPRs in particular as these are the ones incurring further costs (going beyond the research and development costs) to obtain, to

© The Author(s) 2018   33
D. Modic, N. Damij, *Towards Intellectual Property Rights Management*, https://doi.org/10.1007/978-3-319-69011-7_3

maintain, and sometimes to utilize them. Hence, it is important to have before us some discoveries of earlier studies and theoretical contributions to be able to comprehend how to immerse ourselves into this topic. Ziedonis (2008), looking at the highly cited articles, identifies the themes and topics those scholarly contributions explore in the field of IPR: *first* is the use of patents to examine firm capabilities—looking into how technical capabilities are being exploited, competitive advantages developed, and knowledge transferred. However, the *second* identified theme is the use of intellectual property as a strategic asset (with the third being the effects of law and policies towards IP on the innovation incentives). She argues that the value of additional research on IP will *inter alia* come from studies on how companies use IP as strategic assets. Today the revised strategies of patenting and the connected increase of strategic handling of intellectual property (Modic 2013; Neuheussler 2009; Hall and Ziedonis 2001; Cohen et al. 2000) underline the rise of intellectual property applications. However, yielding positive outcomes from intellectual property rights is not a given in this world of patent (or broader IPR) paradox.

IPRs can be used for offensive and/or defensive and/or leveraging purposes (for a short case-in-point, see Box 3.1). As we have already mentioned, some innovation potentials of IPRs and of IPR management are easier to construct than others. They can either contribute to the business or the customers. Looking at many patent disputes by larger companies, we have no doubt IPRs are beneficial to securing the advantage of those owning them and having sufficient funds to pursue breaches by other firms.

Box 3.1 Between offensive and defensive strategies: Patent fences and patent thickness in action or from Nylon to smartphones
Patents may be used both defensively and offensively. In general, "defensive patenting refers to the practice of seeking patents in order to defend oneself from patent infringement actions brought by others" (Shapiro 2004). On the other hand, an offensive patent strategy builds barriers to block competitors from gaining entry to company's proprietary technologies and who are often also not afraid to use them. When companies are asked why and how they use patents, many of them indeed indicate that many of them do so to block rivals (see a number of research endeavours unveiling why companies use patents starting from Cohen et al. 2000); nonetheless this may be done in more defensive or offensive way.

One way to try to block competitors is by using a fence of substitute patents or a thicket of complementary patents. Whereas a (true and problematic) patent fence is often described as a portfolio of (non-improving) substitute patents (Schneider 2005), a definition of a patent thickness is "a dense web of overlapping intellectual property rights that a company must hack its way through in order to actually commercialize new technology" (Shapiro 2000).

Let us take a look at two examples, an older and a newer one. A case of a patent fence is that of DuPont and Nylon. In DuPont, Dr. Carothers discovered nylon, the world's first true synthetic fibre. The first patent was issued in 1938 and the company kept quiet about the innovation until then. During his time with DuPont, Dr. Carothers filed for more than 50 patents (DuPont 2016), but it did not stop there. DuPont filed more than 200 substitutes for Nylon (cited in Cohen et al. 2000).

You must of heard it before: there are estimates that there are more than 250,000 active patents relevant to today's smartphones, which is a significant increase compared to the estimate of approximately 70,000 patents that were active and relevant to mobile phones in 2000 (done by a patent aggregator firm RSX). In such a patent thickness, companies are in the situation where they need to negotiate with other companies to get access to technologies they need; for example, Samsung needs licences from Motorola and Apple. Since other companies also need licences, they end up granting cross-licences. However, it is really not a balanced game, as the size of the portfolios and also the strength of the players can make some "pay a higher price" than others. In a dispute situation, some companies also come on stronger to some competitors than others; consider this statement by the late Steve Jobs: "I will spend every penny of Apple's $40 billion in the bank, to right this wrong. I'm going to destroy Android, because it's a stolen product. I'm willing to go thermonuclear war on this" (BBC News 2011). Nonetheless, it's not all bad news. A recent study by Reidenberg et al. (2015), done for WIPO, showed that patent litigation, whether from operating companies or NPEs, does not appear as a significant concern for small players and does not appear to pose barriers to entry.

Sources:

Shapiro, C. (2004). Technology cross-licensing practices: Ftc v. intel (1999). In *The antitrust revolution: Economics, competition, and policy* (pp. 350–372).

Shapiro, C. (2000). Navigating the patent thicket: Cross licenses, patent pools, and standard setting. In *Innovation policy and the economy* (pp. 119–150).

Dupont. (2016). Nylon milestones. Retrieved from http://www.dupont.com/products-and-services/plastics-polymers-resins/thermoplastics/videos/nylon-milestones.html

American Chemical Society. (1995). *The first nylon plant*. Washington: ACS.

Schneider, C. (2005). Fences and competition in patent races. Retrieved from http://citeseerx.ist.psu.edu/viewdoc/download?doi=10.1.1.555.5470&rep=rep1&type=pdf

RSX Report. (2011). Retrieved from https://www.sec.gov/Archives/edgar/data/1509432/000119312511240287/ds1.htm

BBC News. (2011). Steve Jobs vowed to 'destroy' Android. Retrieved from http://www.bbc.com/news/technology-15400984

Reidenberg, J. R., Russell, C. N., Price, M., & Mohan, A. (2015). *Patents and small participants in the smartphone industry*. Geneva: WIPO.

But how can IPRs and IPR management be beneficial to the customer? Taking the already mentioned example of McDonald's and its franchise holder, we can easily see the benefit of the McDonald's trademark (and the vigorous defence of it by the multinational) for the franchise holder— and similar situations can be seen in most B2B situations.

Other benefits are perhaps less identifiable at first glance. Providing that the IPR process is truly both integrated and aligned, it can lead to a broader or different application or a change in the intended solution, which can render benefits for the business. For example, the contribution by the patent attorney, as one of our interviewees pointed out, can lead to broadening the scope of the applicability of a certain solution, since an integrated procedure may bring also business and legal insights in addition to (perhaps narrower) technical solution.

One of the major problems of intellectual property rights is that the link between using IPRs and the increase of the firm's profitability and the IPR use seems to be lacking. Hence, IPRs may be described as probabilistic at best (Lemley and Shapiro 2005; Chou and Haller 2008). Inside intellectual property rights processes (IPR management), there is a high level of uncertainty present. In general uncertainties stem from incomplete or missing information, which make it impossible to forecast future events, limit informed decisions, and prevent (complete) control over results (Dosi and Egidi 2000). Following Troy and Werle (2008), two types of uncertainties come to play: so-called fundamental uncertainty—referring to the lack of necessary information in the system as a whole—and the so-called strategic uncertainty referring to the asymmetrical dispersion of necessary information. The results of innovation as well as the result of the use of intellectual property protection mechanisms are under the influence of (at least) the following uncertainties: uncertainty associated with R&D activities, uncertainty related to the novelty of the innovation, uncertainty associated with the projection of market needs in conjunction with the uncertainty of valuation, uncertainty arising from the application procedures of the intellectual property rights or those arising from formal conditions related to the use of informal protection mechanisms, uncertainty associated with the failure of the intellectual property markets, and uncertainty associated with the protection of intellectual property (see also Troy and Werle 2008). Hence, a structured, systematic dealing with both innovation processes and intellectual property protection (as the legal reflection of innovation) tends to decrease the level of uncertainty, and *managing risks* is strongly ingrained in IPR management.

To conclude, the most important objective of IP management is to ensure that the IP is being used to its fullest extent and serves to maximize profitability or other business-related opportunities. The IPR process is a sequence of activities through which companies or individuals maintain and exploit their patents, designs, trademarks, copyrights, and trade secrets. Activities involved in this process can be as simple as obtaining IP rights and keeping them renewed or as complicated as developing an integrated IP strategy and aligning it with business strategies (Harrison and Sullivan 2012)—we take into account all these different levels (see below and Chaps. 5 and 6 for a more practice-oriented perspective).

A lot of value is connected with IP rights. Some value is explicit, e.g. financial value. Other values are rather hidden; because IPRs are, for example, protecting a competitive advantage. Therefore, we need to examine for example: What to patent? When to patent? Where to patent? How long to maintain the patent? These strategic decisions are an important part of the IPR management.
Chief IP Counsel,
German conglomerate manufacturing and electronics company

Looking at IPR management, there are two different levels or dimensions we need to pay attention to. *Firstly*, is the IPR process on the level of individual IPR right (we talk about them more from a practical point of view especially in Chap. 6 and the end part of Chap. 7)? *Secondly*, there is the strategic level—building a framework for handling IPR (we also dedicate a section on this in Chap. 6 with the emphasis by our interviewees). Companies have different overall IPR strategies (depending on their size, sector they operate in, age, etc.), and they also tend to change throughout the evolution of the firm (consider also the case in Box 3.2).

Box 3.2 The patent portfolio insight from Facebook: A story of evolution
Facebook had very few patents in its initial years of operations, but by now that has changed to a large degree (histories of Amazon or Twitter show a very similar path). But Facebook does not rely on filing patents by itself. In 2012 TechCrunch reported that only approximately 3% of Facebook's patents were originally filed by Facebook. Facebook, however, had a portfolio of about 2233 US patents in 2016 and 30% of them were not acquired elsewhere. The recently released USPTO Patent Assignment Database shows, for example, a tad over 2000 cases where Facebook was the assignee (relating to assignments from its own current or former employees or other companies). Amazon appears more than 4000 times. Twitter started its "patent pledge" in 2013 with as little as two patents. Its portfolio grew to more than 900 patents by 2016 (similarly to Facebook, with only 2% of patents originally filed by Twitter). Nonetheless, in recent years, Facebook has consistently looked to the outside in order to augment its IP position with strategic acquisitions of patents.

It is well known that prospective litigation was the driver behind the acquisition of many IPRs, especially those from IBM (again, similar can be said for Twitter). These acquisitions provide Facebook with access to IP that is significantly older than its own IP by seeking out valuable "Not Invented Here" IPR. Older patents are subject to fewer prior art and are thus easier to defend against, as well as provide leverage for the asserting party, by allowing the collection of up to six years of damages from the infringer. But the evolution of business directs the evolution of IP portfolios as well. Hence, when Facebook realized that Google was being a direct competitor for IP assets in some areas, it needed to take measures. This needed to be done, not only with today's needs in mind (partnering with Microsoft and acquiring their AOL patent portfolio) but also with an eye for where the company will be developing in the future (see Facebook's attempts to join the mobile phone markets by partnering with HTC). Because constant augmenting of its IP portfolio helps to increase the value of Facebook, more acquisitions are likely to take place. According to the patent bases, however, Facebook's own number of filings is also increasing. In time Facebook may also be going more in the direction taken by Amazon, attempting to enhance its leadership and diversification.

Sources:

USPTO Patent Assignment Database. Retrieved from http://assignment.uspto.gov/

USPTO Patent Database. Retrieved from http://patft.uspto.gov/

Kravets, L. (2012). Facebook's patent acquisitions? They're more about Google than Yahoo. *Techcrunch*, April 27, 2012. Retrieved from https://techcrunch.com/2012/04/27/facebook-google-patents/

Leemay, A. (2016). Twitter grows its patent portfolio via acquisitions. *Patentvue*, May 30, 2016. Retrieved from http://patentvue.com/2016/05/30/twitter-grows-its-patent-portfolio-via-acquisitions/

Quinn G., & Brachmann, S. (2014). Facebook and Twitter: Patent strategies for social media. *IPWatchdog*, February 14, 2014. Retrieved from http://www.ipwatchdog.com/2014/02/14/facebook-and-twitter-patent-strategies-for-social-media/id=48004/

GB. (2017). Amazon & Facebook—Patent portfolio insights. Retrieved from http://www.greyb.com/amazon-facebook-patent-portfolio-insights/

Theoretically, we can find several typologies of IPR strategies: (a) those defined by the overall goal (defensive, offensive, and leveraging strategy[1]), (b) those defined by the type of IP(R) asset (patent, design, trademark, copyright, trade secret strategy), (c) those defined by the stage or IPR sub-process (e.g. registration, licensing, enforcement strategy), or (d) those defined by the type of activities (external or internal[2]). In practice, we need to note two things: firstly, the IPR strategy will mostly be subsumed into the IP strategy (and both can be either written down (i.e. codified) or not); and secondly, most firms will use (or should use) a combination. Elton et al. (2002) estimate that 10% of the patent portfolio of a R&D intensive company is underexploited and could generate approximately 5% of the operating income via licensing. This tells us that even a R&D intensive company should not stick solely to a strategy favouring only stopping others occupying their (intended) technology (or better: market) space— that is, offensive strategy. Although the company needs to develop guidelines in which cases benefitting from, for example, licensing can occur (thus using a defensive or leveraging strategy). On the other hand, so-called non-practicing entities (here having in mind especially the patent trolls) might pursue only a specific strategy also due to their overall business model.

> The basis for our IP process is—what I call—a Framework IP Strategy, which is binding for our entire group. We regularly review it; answering the question whether it is still up to date. We make necessary changes if needed and then also devise necessary changes to IP processes.
> Chief IP Counsel,
> German conglomerate manufacturing and electronics company

We can also look at this issue from a different viewpoint of evolution of the IPR "strategies" (on the lowest level perhaps the term of simply handling IPR is more appropriate), where companies go from treating the IPRs as legal assets or as business assets. Harrison and Sullivan (2012) have proposed a value hierarchy illuminating different expectations on the contribution of the IP(R) on overall company goals. The first level is the "defend position"—providing patent shields or IPT shield is how they see the IPR main contribution. Next is the manage costs level, where the foci are in (by still achieving the defend position) lowering the costs connected to IPRs (e.g. we will later on also look at the importance of pruning). But to really be able to think about IPR management as business process management, the level of "capture value" should be achieved—where companies are proactively finding new goals for the IPR and seeing IPR as a business asset. Next is the synthesize opportunities level according to Harrison and Sullivan (2012) seeing IPRs as strategic assets as well— bringing us to the multilayer IPRM structure of IPR management of individual IPR processes as well as the strategic level. The focus is now not only on the IPR as such but on the process. The last level is the "shape the future" level—most of our interviewees come from firms which are able to recognize future needs and trends (both their own and those inside their business milieu).

Hence, on one hand, a thorough understanding of the IPR process is needed to employ any of the above-mentioned strategies; and on the other hand, a change in the strategic goals can cause changes in IPR process, as they need to adapt.

All of this furthers our notion that the intellectual property protection processes need to be systematic, carefully designed, and thoroughly thought through. Thus, it is of utmost importance that the IPR processes are carried out and designed as diligently as possible (Modic and Damij 2016) while taking into account all the gaps and trying to avoid as many pitfalls as possible.

3.2   IPR Processes as Business Processes: A Theoretical Perspective

Innovation and entrepreneurship are tightly interconnected, since for companies the final desired outcome is profit. Therefore, to achieve this outcome, it is required that innovation be organized as a systematic activity (Drucker 2010), which is especially true for the processes of intellectual property protection (IPP). Generally, processes are understood as transformations of inputs to outputs (Laguna and Marklund 2005) or defined as structured, measured sets of activities designed to produce a specified output for a particular customer or market (Davenport 1993). During the transformation or measured sets of activities, inputs are developed into value-added outputs. As such, it is inputs and consequently outputs such as IPRs that define the relationships between the organization and the outside world. Processes, IPP in particular, rely strongly on human resources (labour) and the activities they are tasked to do. According to Laguna and Marklund (2005), resources are origins of supply, material assets required to activate process activities, and are consequently twofold: capital assets and labour. Human resources and their allocation to specific tasks and activities transform inputs into value-added outputs through executing a series of activities sequentially and/or linked in parallel. Activities themselves are exploited within the process but not consumed (Damij 2007).

A business process (BP) is as a collection of activities that takes one or more kinds of input and creates an output that is of a value to the customer (Hammer 1990). The value-added outputs are closely related to the organizations' strategic aims and goals. Furthermore, as BPs focus on how activities are interlinked and executed, they demonstrate, in detail, an agile resume of an organization and its functioning. The agility of business processes is closely related to the changes within organizations, but even more with the changes in the outside world in which the organizations function and which is measuring the added values of the organizations' outputs. Agile resumes consequently enable organizations to acquire a better ability to concentrate on BPs execution as well as add value to outputs being sent to the outside world. Such an approach enables organizations to discover the true demands and desires of the consumers rather than spending time dealing with internal matters such as organizational structure or business rules (Ackermann et al. 1999). This is especially true in IPR processes as IPRs ought to be carefully designed and thoroughly thought through.

Are IPR processes really business processes? Based on the Hammer (1990) definition, what are the inputs of intellectual property protection processes? How, if at all, are the inputs transformed into outputs and do outputs have added values? For whom?

Much was written on how to accomplish the maximum outputs of intellectual property rights (IPRs)—and intellectual property (IP) more broadly—however, the "know-how" and actual tools to achieve them seem to still be lacking a decade and a half after Rivette and Kline wrote that the patent asset management is (or should be) a new corporate strategy issue and that the world's most successful companies regard patent strategy as a "new core competency of a modern enterprise and an important factor in their success" (Rivette and Kline 2000). This is especially true for small-sized companies where the optimization of their IPR processes is still often more of an idea than an actual practice (Modic and Damij 2016). IPR processes as business processes enable companies to adapt to an ever-changing environment in which companies function using a threefold approach, through the preparation, exploitation, and violation elimination phase. The goal of the preparation phase is to obtain an intellectual property and develop a protection mechanism; the goals of the exploitation phase are to focus on the market and the IPR market with its strategic use as secondary, whereas the goals of the (optional) violation elimination phase deal with a discovery of a violation of their IP. Kock and McQueen (1998) concur with the categorization of business processes by three types, however, rather than the management processes (as the third type). They see the need to include the improvement processes as they are, when linked with the core and support processes, the ones where knowledge exchange happens. We further explore the distinction between core and support processes in regard to the IPRM business processes in Chap. 5.

IPR processes need to be systematic, carefully designed, and thoroughly thought through, especially during the preparation phase as processes are designed as diligently as possible (Modic and Damij 2016) following firstly the identification of their activities and secondly the sequence of the latter (Damij 2007) by focusing on including all required information and elements about the process, its inputs and more importantly the value-added outputs, and any additional data required for the so-called product lifecycle management as seen in Chap. 6.

3.3   BUSINESS MODEL AND MODELLING

Even though many good real-world practices as well as extensive publications exist and are publicly available, the field of business process modelling is still not mastered or integrated into companies' processes. Some companies—small-, medium-, or large-sized ones—are not fully exploring the pros of using various business process modelling approaches when structuring their activities. The aim of using the business process model is to identify activities that need to be carried out in order for the company to produce a service or a product, whose value is consequently recognized by the consumer. Additionally, integrating business process modelling approaches into a company's behaviour also identifies bottlenecks and promotes business process improvements, thus ensuring required process changes are recognized and implemented. Various business process modelling approaches, methods, techniques, and methodologies exist, and it is up to the company to identify the one or a combination of them that best suit their behaviour.

The literature review clearly shows that the field of business process modelling has gained acknowledgement by scientific and applied societies, as literature, academic publications, white papers, and so on can be found as well as companies providing consultancies in the area have been on the increase in the past three or four decades. Various researches examining, comparing, and contrasting different business process modelling approaches can be found (Damij 2007). A complete understanding and identification of business processes within an organization can consequently lead to effective, efficient, and value-added systems. The conceptual modelling of business processes is deployed on a large scale to facilitate the development of software that supports the business processes and to permit the analysis and re-engineering or improvement of them (Aguilar-Saven 2003).

Even though many good real-world practices as well as extensive publications exist and are publicly available, the field of business process modelling is still not mastered or integrated into companies' processes. Some companies, small, medium, or large size ones, are not fully exploring the pros of using various business process modelling approaches when structuring their activities. The aim of using the business process model is to identify activities that need to be carried out in order for the company to produce a service or a product, whose value is consequently recognized by the consumer. Additionally, integrating business process modelling approaches into a company's behaviour also identifies bottlenecks and promotes business process improvements, thus ensuring required process changes are recognized and implemented. Various business process modelling approaches, methods, techniques, and methodologies exist, and it is up to the company to identify the one or combination of ones that best suit their behaviour (consult Box 3.3).

Box 3.3 Huawei's approach to IPR process management

The company's IPR department was established in the mid-1990s and has since then grown to over 100 employees with the aim to monitor and master the competitors' outputs based on intellectual property applications. Their approach is mainly defensive, predominantly focusing on advancements of western ICT products and services, resulting in acquisition of IPRs that enable the company to benefit from the already developed ICTs. Consequently, many of their IPR applications are submitted as subservient patents and utilized for leveraging in cross-licensing. The employees are heavily present at all major international conferences and workshops to further grasp the advances in their field. Furthermore, Huawei's (IPR) processes are supported by the company's high annual investments in their R&D departments (10%) that enable them, among others, to employ a vast number of researchers.

Huawei's global presence is felt strongly. Their approach is conservative and has many times included the development of strategic partnerships for the geographical area they wanted to pursue, enabling them to develop a major global R&D network of partnerships (Microsoft, Siemens, Motorola, IBM, Intel, Agere Systems, Altera, Qualcomm, etc.). The company's business processes as well as some of their products are defined to fully support such strategies. For example, Huawei's standard business process framework is defined as a promoter of business operations, functions, and process improvement and/or redesign. It is believed to revolutionize the management of processes, the way business is conducted, the efficiency achieved by embracing the "correct" processes, softwares, hardwares, and human resources, all with the aim of adopting and implementing future services and value chains.

Sources:

Donglin, W., & Fang, Z. (2007). Entry modes for international markets: Case study of Huawei, a Chinese technology enterprise. Retrieved from https://www.researchgate.net/profile/Fang_Zhao14/publication/228646096_Entry_Modes_For_International_Markets_Case_Study_Of_Huawei_A_Chinese_Technology_Enterprise/links/55375d1d0cf2058efdeab879/Entry-Modes-For-International-Markets-Case-Study-Of-Huawei-A-Chinese-Technology-Enterprise.pdf

Nakai, Y., & Tanaka, Y. (2010). Chinese company's IPR strategy: Hoe Huawei technologies succeeded in dominating overseas market by sideward-crawl strategy. Retrieved from http://ieeexplore.ieee.org/abstract/document/5602172/

Dickson, K., & Fang, F. Management of R&D within dynamic standardization environment. Retrieved from http://www4.pucsp.br/icim2009/ingles/downloads/pdf_proceedings_2008/53.pdf

Business process modelling approaches and their successful implementation/deployment within the companies rely on selecting one or more of the most suitable modelling methods or techniques or, as is the case of some large multinational companies, developing their own techniques. There are various business process modelling techniques available such as general process charts, process activity charts, flowcharts, dataflow diagrams, quality function deployment, the integrated definition of function modelling, coloured Petri nets, object-oriented methods, seven management and planning tools, and so on. Their aims are not only to identify or monitor activities required to, for example, develop a product or service but also to identify major problems or challenges within the process.

3.4   TAD as IPR Modelling Tool

TAD methodology dates back to 1998 and has since then has seen various updates mainly focusing on its application to various areas (e.g. sales processes, health processes, service industry), not only for information system/software development that was its initial focus. TAD methodology consists of six phases (either linked or stand-alone); however, for the purpose of IPR process analysis, only part of the methodology that is directly linked to business process development and analysis will be used. The second phase of TAD methodology deals specifically with business process identification and development using a tool called the Activity Table. We will be only using the Activity Table as an IPR modelling tool for business process analysis.

As mentioned, TAD methodology consists of six phases. The first phase investigates an organization's problems, specifically focusing on their business process identification and problems related to them. The identification of business processes presents a big challenge; however, it strongly correlates with the organization's level of maturity, meaning the greater level of maturity of the organization, the better knowledge of their business processes lies within the organization. Nonetheless, the business process identification must be executed rigorously as it lays the foundation for the subsequent five phases of the methodology such as business process modelling, improvement/innovation, system development, and implementation.

On a day-to-day basis, organizations deal with a large number of processes, all diverse in scope, size, and complexity, and linked to each other in a specific way. The number of stakeholders involved in these processes varies, thus decreasing or increasing the level of bottlenecks, inefficiencies, and delays with the process executing the production of the output (a product or service). Davenport (1993) illustrated some of the challenges of organizations such as IBM and Xerox, where at the time of his research both have described to have a large number of processes running within the companies (IBM identified over 140 processes); however, with the focus on the business process identification where the key attribute of a business process is the transformation of the input into the output, he defined only 14 business processes in Xerox and 18 business processes in IBM, thus increasing their level of awareness and maturity.

The Activity Table tool is the main part of the second phase of TAD methodology and focuses on identifying business process(es) by presenting the activities within each process, establishing their sequence, and linking them with the resources/entities/stakeholders responsible for carrying out/performing/executing them. By doing so, an "as-is" model is created to capture the behaviour the process in a way to as closely as possible simulate the functioning of the actual business process. When the Activity Table tool was first introduced by Damij (1998), it enabled two ways for the "as-is" model creation—either using letters to present the sequence of activities and their entities or presenting them graphically with the use of various symbols. Through the years the tabular graphical presentation has been more widely used as it enabled all stakeholders to understand and view the process being analyzed without any previous knowledge of the methodology itself. Such an approach enabled a link between the resources and each specific activity: the first being presented in the columns and the latter in the rows of the table. All of them need to be linked in some way—either presenting the successive or parallel connections. The Activity Table presents one or more business processes, each of them consisting of a series of work processes and/or sub-processes (the sub-processes identified are listed in the second column of the Activity Table (Damij 1998)), that are further divided into a set of linked activities (the activities identified are listed in the third column of the Activity Table). Hence, the name—the Activity Table. Simultaneously with defining the content of the second column, the content of the first row of the Activity Table is created by entering the names of those departments in which the work processes listed are performed (Damij et al. 2008). All required information is gained through the execution of interviews with the key stakeholders in order to identify (Damij et al. 2008):

1. the sequence of the work processes by linking them to the business process.
2. the human resources responsible for the identified work processes.
3. the sequence of the activities carried out within the identified work processes.

Every activity identified is linked on at least one predecessor and at least one successor activity. The exemptions are only the starting and ending activities, where the starting activity has no predecessor activity and the ending activity has no successor activity. Furthermore, it is not only business processes that are linked to their inputs and outputs—the same is applied to each activity, meaning that for every activity (more or less) an input and output need to be identified. The activities are linked together using arrows—the direction in which the arrow points is the direction of the process flow. The flow (arrows) can be twofold: the horizontal ones connect the activity with the human resource(s) executing the activity, whereas the vertical ones connect the activity to its successor activity(ies). For further use and implementation of the Activity Table modelling tool, please refer to Chap. 7, where the generic IPRM process model is presented by using the Activity Table technique.

In order to understand the Activity Table model, the following set of symbols are also used to assist the relevant stakeholders by giving a thorough understanding of the process model (Damij 1998):

- Symbol ○ indicates the starting point of a process.
- Symbol ⊙ indicates the endpoint of a process or the end of a certain path of the process.
- Symbol □ in cell (i,j) means that resource (j) performs activity (i), where j ranges from 1 to the number of resources and i ranges from 1 to the number of activities.
- Symbol ◊ in cell (i,j) means that activity (i) is a decision activity. Such an activity starts different alternative paths and is succeeded by different alternative successor activities.
- Horizontal arrows are used to connect the activity horizontally. A horizontal arrow that is drawn from cell (i,j) to cell (i, k) shows a horizontal linkage from activity (i), which is performed by the resource (j), to resource (k), which is related to the activity's output.

- Vertical arrows are used to link the activities vertically. A vertical arrow that is drawn from cell (i,j) to cell (k, j) shows a vertical linkage from activity (i) to its successor activity (k).

Either before or at the same time, another part of the Activity Table is developed in order to fully develop the process model of the business process under investigation. This part is mainly focused on the process behaviour—the process model can only be as good as the description of the business process discussed. In order to thoroughly describe the business process, additional information regarding each activity is required, such as Damij et al. (2008):

- A precise and short description of the activity,
- Input(s) that triggers the processing of the activity,
- Output(s) created by processing the activity,
- Constraints and rules related to the activity's execution,
- The duration of time estimated for performing the activity, and
- Resources needed for the performing of the activity or related to the activity.
- Cost. This is the sum of the expenses needed to accomplish activity (i). This parameter is later used to calculate the cost of each work process and consequently the whole business process. Thus, this is an important parameter that needs to be calculated for the purpose of business process improvement and innovation.

In reality, not all the above-mentioned elements are available for every business process; cost and duration especially are elements that are rarely measured on the level of each activity (focusing on service processes). However, their understanding is important for the full understanding of the business process under review. Often though, these elements of the Activity Table are presented separately (and not within the same table), purely due to space limitations. For further reading on these and the generic IPRM process model including these elements, refer to Chap. 6.

The aim of this chapter was to look closely at the IPR processes on one hand and business processes on the other. Furthermore, we tried to identify the IPRM processes as business processes by evaluating them through key business process elements such as IPRM process inputs, outputs, activity description and sequencing, as well as resource allocation that consequently enable the development of IPR process models. By doing so, we also looked at different business process definitions in order to set foundations for the empirical research in the following chapters. The modelling of IPR processes is presented by the use of the TAD modelling approach and the steps necessary to transform the IPRM process into a business process model. Both business process modelling and the Activity Table technique are used to identify the value-added IPRM process outputs and, if necessary, refocus the IPR process to achieve this. We are trying to see if in practice we can indeed speak of a *sui generis* field of IPR management. The alternative being that IPR management is so entangled in other processes and activities that we can simply not see it as a standalone. We believe that the laid-out approach in this chapter as well as its empirical application in the following chapters will promote further encouragement especially for smaller organizations to perhaps try to exploit IPRM processes and the development of the IPRs.

NOTES

1. A proprietary strategy is the logic of using patents as isolating or deflecting mechanisms, shielding the firm's key competitive advantages from imitation. This can be done by exploiting IPR through the goods market (i.e. putting the product on the market) or through the market for ideas (e.g. licensing). It will usually be connected to terms such as building fences, "offensive" blocking and pre-emption, building "offensive" thickets (Somaya 2012). A defensive strategy is, simply put, a strategy for defending against patents owned (and enforced) by others. Hence, it is directed towards stopping others from occupying a certain market/technological space. Another note: while the use of the term defensive (as used by practitioners) may appear to be similar to a defensive patent strategy, companies sometimes need to assert their "defensive patents"—that is, go on the offensive—if the defensive strategy is to be credible (Somaya 2003). Lastly, if the company sees IPRs as bargaining chips, we are talking about a leveraging strategy. This strategy is all about pursuing direct or indirect profit opportunities; we may see this connected to terms like cross-licensing, patent pools, signalling, IPR-based cooperation, entry to a new market, standard setting.
2. Pithelky (2001) also sees IPRM tactical and strategic issues—the latter a concern of senior IP managers—split into internal and external. The first envelops issues that are internal to the company (e.g. IPR registration, issues regarding confidentiality, and raising IP awareness) and the second issues concerning licensing, IP information, and litigation.

REFERENCES

Ackerman, F., Walls, L., Meer, R., & Boorman, M. (1999). Taking a strategic view of BPR to develop a multidisciplinary framework. *Journal of Operational Research Society, 50*(3), 195–204.

Aguilar-Saven, R., & Olhager, J. (2003). Integration of product, process and functional orientations: Principles and a case study. In H. S. Jagdev, J. C. Wortmann, & H. J. Pels (Eds.), *Collaborative systems for production management.* Vol. 129 of IFIP—The International Federation for Information Processing (pp. 375–389). Springer US.

Chou, T., & Haller, H. (2008). Reasonable royalty and the division of profit for probabilistic patents. *ASLEA Papers.* Retrieved May 15, 2014, from http://www.en.kyushu-u.ac.jp/aslea/apapers/AsLEA-2008-TeyuChou.pdf

Cohen, W. M., Nelson, R. R., & Walsh, J. P. (2000). Protecting their intellectual assets: Appropriability conditions and why U.S. manufacturing firms patent (or not). Cambridge, MA: NBER.

Damij, N. (2007). Business process modelling using diagrammatic and tabular techniques. *Business Process Management Journal, 13*(1), 70–90.

Damij, N., Damij, T., Grad, J., & Jelenc, F. (2008). A methodology for business process improvement and IS development. *Information and Software Technology, 50*, 1127–1141.

Damij, T. (1998). Development of a hospital information system using the TAD method. *Journal of American Medical Informatics Association, 5*, 184–193.

Davenport, T. H. (1993). *Process innovation: Reengineering work through information technology.* Boston, MA: Harvard Business School Press.

Dosi, G., & Egidi, M. (2000). Substantive and procedural uncertainty. In G. Dosi (Ed.), *Innovation, market organization and economic dynamics: Selected essays* (pp. 165–188). Cheltenham and Northampton: Edward Elgar Publishing.

Drucker, P. F. (2010). *Innovation and entrepreneurship.* Oxford and Burlington: Elsevier.

Elton, J., Shah, B., & Voyzey, J. (2002). Intellectual property: Partnering for profit. *The McKinsey Quarterly, 4*(2002), 59–67.

Hall, B., & Ziedonis, H. R. (2001). The patent paradox revisited: An empirical study of patenting in the U.S. semiconductor industry, 1979–1995. *The RAND Journal of Economics, 32*(1), 101–128.

Hammer, M. (1990). Reengineering work: Don't automate, obliterate. *Harvard Business Review, 90*(4), 104–112.

Harrison, S. S., & Sullivan, P. H. (2012). *Edison in the boardroom revisited: How leading companies realize value from their intellectual property: Revisited.* Hoboken, NJ: Wiley.

Kock, N., & McQueen, R. J. (1998). An action research case-study of effects of asynchronous groupware support on productivity and outcome quality of process redesign groups. *Journal of Organizational Computing and Electronic Commerce, 8*(2), 149–168.

Laguna, M., & Marklund, J. (2005). *Business process modeling, simulation, and design*. New Jersey: Pearson Education, Inc.

Lemley, M. A., & Shapiro, C. (2005). Probabilistic patents. *Journal of Economic Perspectives, 19*(2), 75–98.

Modic, D. (2013). *New views on intellectual property protection in the context of innovation systems (in case of Slovenia)*. Dissertation, Faculty of Advanced Social Sciences.

Modic, D., & Damij, N. (2016). "Own-it": Managing intellectual property processes via the activity table in creative industries. In A. Lugmayr, E. Stojmenova, K. Stanoevska, & R. Wellington (Eds.), *Information systems and management in eMedia industry* (pp. 101–117). Cham: Springer.

Neuheusler, P. (2009). *Formal vs. informal protection instruments and the strategic use of patents in an Expected-Utility framework*. Fraunhofer ISI Discussion Papers Innovation Systems and Policy Analysis, No. 20, Fraunhofer ISI, Karlsruhe.

Pithelky, R. H. (2001). Intellectual property strategy in Japanese and UK companies: Patent licensing decisions and learning opportunities. *Research Policy, 30*, 425–442.

Rivette, K. G., & Kline, D. (2000). *Rembrandts in the attic: Unlocking the hidden value of patents*. Boston: Harvard Business School Press.

Somaya, D. (2003). Strategic determinants of decision not to settle patent litigation. *Strategic Management Journal, 24*, 17.

Somaya, D. (2012). Patent strategy and management: An integrative review and research agenda. *Journal of Management, 38*(4), 1084–1114.

Troy, I., & Werle, R. (2008). *Uncertainty and market for patents*. MPIfG Working Paper 08/2, Max Plank Institute for the Study of Societies, Cologne (pp. 1–24).

Ziedonis, R. H. (2008). Intellectual property and innovation. In *Handbook of technology and innovation management* (pp. 295–334).

Interviewing IPR Executives

Abstract We start the empirical part of this book by asking the question: How can a move from IPR management to business management be accomplished? Chapter 4 is thus a short methodological review describing the empirical approach we employed, our comments regarding select interviewees, connected processes of data gathering and data analysis.

We have divided this chapter into three parts: "Who to ask and why?" in order to demonstrate relevance of the interviewees, that is, top IP executives from IPR savvy multinational companies; "How did we do it?" in order to define the research protocol; and finally, "Why hasn't it been done before?" illustrating the difficulties one faces when conducting this type of research.

Keywords IPR experts interviews • IPR research methodology • IPR savvy companies

As an introductory chapter to the subsequent three chapters that present the results of interviews in this chapter, we answer these three questions: (a) Who to ask and why? (b) How did we do it? and (c) Why hasn't it been done before? We start with the description of the research framework, followed by the description of our research approach, and finally, examining factors hindering this type of research.

4.1   Who to Ask and Why?

Let us stress this once again: IPR management is not easy. That is why the short answer to the question of who to interview is, in our opinion, IP executives who have ample experience with the different aspects of managing intellectual property rights and work at IPR savvy multinationals.

The research we conducted has engaged top IP executives (see Table 4.1). Interviews were conducted throughout 2016. In total, ten prominent IP experts were interviewed. Seven of them are head IP managers in their respective companies. They are individuals whose main tasks/responsibilities are related to so-called Front-office, but who have sufficient overview and (for the most part) bear the responsibility for coordination of Back-office operations as well. This allows us to gain a holistic overview. Some of the executives, and the companies they work for, wished to remain anonymous, others agreed to be named, such as Mr. Beat Weibel, Senior Vice-President and Chief IP Counsel at Siemens. All of them are executives with many years of experience; for example, one of the interviewees was twice voted within the 50 most influential people in IP by Managing Intellectual Property magazine (MIP)—Mr. Gerhard Bauer. Inside the monograph we always name their titles and the descriptive naming of the company they come from.

The experts are affiliated with companies that have ranked in top spots in terms of both patent applications and rankings of quality such as the Patent Asset Index (by PatentSight). Furthermore, we can find them on the lists of the world's top innovators, such as among MIT's list of 50 smartest companies. The views expressed inside the interviews are their own and not the views of the companies they are affiliated with.

Innovation seems to differ substantially across sectors in terms of "characteristics, sources, actors involved, boundaries of the process, and the organization of innovative activities" (Malerba 2006). When looking at intellectual property rights, variability is also noticeable when we compare different sectors of the economy. Variability in IPR management can also be seen among companies operating within the same sector (as we have learned in our interviews; on a more general level, you can see indications of this in OECD 2015).

Until recently protecting IPR was seen primarily as something technology and pharmaceutical companies engage in and not something a "normal" company needs to concern itself with. However, these times seem to be over. An interesting example is that of the CEO of MasterCard, Ajay

Table 4.1   List of respondents

Title	Affiliation description	Additional details
Head of Legal Operations and IP Management	European multinational pharmaceutical company	One of the ten largest pharma companies in the world *More than 50,000 patent applications*
Senior Vice-President, Chief IP Counsel	German conglomerate manufacturing and electronics company	One of the biggest electronics companies in the world *More than 50,000 patent applications*
Chief IP Counsel	German international automotive supplier	The company has more than 60 sites in over 20 countries *Between 500 and 10,000 patent applications*
Ex-Chief Trademark Counsel (also: IP consultant and former Head of BusinessEurope's Working Group on Trademarks and Designs)	German multinational automotive corporation	The company has affiliated companies in the USA and Asia *More than 50,000 patent applications*
Assistant to President of the Board	Slovenian automotive supplier	Headquartered in Novo Mesto, Slovenia *Less than 500 patent applications*
Corporate Patent Manager	Belgian multinational chemical company	The company has affiliated companies on most continents *Between 500 and 10,000 patent applications*
COO of the subsidiary IPR company	German multinational industrial conglomerate	A company with 670 subsidiaries worldwide *Between 500 and 10,000 patent applications*
Chief Intellectual Property Officer	European telecommunication company	European landline and mobile telecommunications company *Less than 500 patent applications*
Director of Licensing Operations	European pharmaceutical company	One of the ten largest pharmaceutical companies in the world *Between 500 and 10,000 patent applications*

(continued)

Table 4.1 (continued)

Title	Affiliation description	Additional details
Senior IP Counsel	German multinational chemicals manufacturing corporation	One of the largest manufacturing companies in the world, with units in more than 80 countries all over the world *More than 50,000 patent applications*

Banga. In 2011 the newly appointed CEO of MasterCard said that MasterCard—a traditional B2B payment company—"is a technology company that's in the payments space" (Levis et al. 2014). In other words, the importance of IPR is growing overall. This is why—although we have sought to interview people from traditionally more active sectors (such as pharma)—we have also included representatives of other sectors, especially those working in information and communication technology (ICT).

Lastly, variability within the same multinational company also deserves to be mentioned, both in terms of diversity of IPR processes between different parts of the company and in terms of time or maturity of the company (as also seen in the case study of Facebook in Chap. 3).

4.2   How Did We Do It?

Based on the literature review, including both theoretical insights and research work results, the threefold questionnaire was designed. The first part included questions regarding the definition of IPR management and its scope. Special emphasis was given to the integration and alignment of IPR management processes with other processes in the company. The second part included questions regarding the formalization and optimization of IPR management processes, questions regarding IPR process innovation, with a special emphasis on critical activities and benchmarking strengths as identified by the respondents. The third part concentrated on two dimensions: firstly, the informational dimension—the use of IPR tools and the prospects of IPR big data analysis—and secondly, on people involved in IPR processes.

In preparation for the interviews, an analysis of web content regarding the prospective interviewees and their respective companies was conducted. Some of the information gathered is included in the following chapters. Furthermore, information gathered from the analysis of internal documentation, which was provided to us by the interviewees, is also integrated.

Interviews were conducted either in person (*inter alia* in Slovenia and Paris, France) or via Skype or similar software tools. Transcripts were analysed using MAXQDA Analytics Pro 12 software in two phases. Phase I included the analysis of definitions, scope, attributes of IPR management. The results of Phase I analysis were used to construct the next chapter of this monograph. Phase II concentrated on activities and people involved in IPR processes. The latter was (together with the related literature review) the basis for the construction of the activity flow and related table delineating the people involved and the characteristics of the activities as well as for the construction of the Activity Table, which was used as an interpretative framework describing the IPR management practices.

Follow-ups were conducted with several interviewees, especially regarding the Activity Table. For the same purpose, additional experts were consulted (see Table 4.2).

They were selected in order to complement the information gained from the interviews (all of them having substantial business experience with IPR processes in larger companies; they, however, are now in different positions) as well as to try to gain some insight and minimize any geographical bias that might have occurred. We also sometimes allude to interviews (and Activity Tables constructed on their basis) with people in charge of IPR management in smaller firms. This, however, is only done for illustrative or comparative purpose, and the interviews in the above-mentioned table themselves are outside the scope of this monograph.

Table 4.2   List of additional experts consulted on activity flow

Position	Affiliation
Patent Attorney, Partner	US-based patent attorney office
Patent Attorney and Professor of Intellectual Property Law	Japanese-based attorney office and university
Director of Business Development Transactions	Chinese-based pharmaceutical company
Consultant	Slovenian-based innovation association
Executive director	US-based Innovation Alliance Accelerator

4.3   WHY HASN'T IT BEEN DONE BEFORE?

We believe the answer to this question is multifold. *Firstly*, the term IP management has been able to permeate the theory and practice to such a degree it hardly leaves any free space for alternatives. *Secondly*, IPR and IPR management have a negative connotation—this often makes people dealing with the field use other terminology.

In addition to the above two reasons, it is not always easy to be able to access a sufficiently large group of top IP executives willing to share their knowledge, insights, and experience. That is not to say there is a lack of either survey-based or (limited) case-based works, where interviewees from IP savvy multinationals were involved in. However, there is either a really limited scope of cases (one or two), which are mostly based on web searches, article analysis, and similar, or we get a rather superficial overview based on broad surveys. Gathering input from IP executives is rare, and gathering input from top IP executives from some of the most IPR savvy multinationals in the world is even rarer. They are usually able to offer insight not only into the experience their respective companies have gained, but many of them have, during their long careers, themselves gained and can share valuable insights from working in various IPR savvy companies.

The focus of this chapter was to introduce the empirical part of the research through a short methodological review demonstrating pertinent experts, the framework of the research protocol, and to identify challenges faced. The next chapter brings a valuable contribution to our knowledge and insights on how top IPR executives manage intellectual property rights.

REFERENCES

Levis, J., Fancher, D., Syed, E., & Hudson, J. (2014). Wizards and trolls: Accelerating technologies, patent reform, and the new era of IP. *Deloitte Review, 2014*(15), 117–133.

Malerba, F. (2006). Innovation and the evolution of industries. *Journal of Evolutionary Economics, 16*(1–2), 3–23.

OECD. (2015). *OECD world corporate top R&D investors: Innovation and IP bundles.* Paris: OECD.

CHAPTER 5

IPR Management to Business Management

Abstract This chapter presents one of the highlights of this book as it draws on the interviews and brings us one step closer to the definition of IPR management rooted in practice. It begins by emphasizing the notion that IPRs are different from other intangibles, especially with regard to their manageability and informational value. The chapter continues by accentuating the IP executives' views of the IPR's benefits.

We also attempt to gain an in-depth view at what differentiates IPR management from IP management. We do this by answering the questions dealing with the justification of IPR management in practice, discovering the companies' IPR management needs by combining interview results with critical literature review.

Keywords Manageability of IPR • IPR management • IP management • IPR management innovation potential • IPR process as business process • IPR core or auxiliary process

Regardless of whom you ask—either an IPR Rookie or practically any of our interviewees who are high-level employees of some of the world's top IPR savvy R&D investor companies—managing IPR is complex. Hence, this is the first chapter that brings the analysis of interviews with IP(R) executives, including some employed by the world's leading multinationals.

© The Author(s) 2018
D. Modic, N. Damij, *Towards Intellectual Property Rights Management*, https://doi.org/10.1007/978-3-319-69011-7_5

We try to get an in-depth insight into what exactly differentiates IPR management (IPRM) from IP management (IPM) and provide an answer to the question of whether or not we are justified to speak of IPR management in practice. Additionally, we aim to discover the needs companies have in connection to IPR management, combining the results of the interviews with critical literature review. We try to identify knowledge gaps and any additional gaps preventing efficient IPR management. Finally, the chapter delineates IPRM from the perspective of the value IPRM outputs add to the company and, as such, identifies IPR process as business process.

The reader will be able to quickly notice the contrast between what is put forward in the literature as the main distinction between IPR and other intangibles and what IPR executives see as their key attributes. For example, what is mostly put at the forefront by top IPR executives are the manageability and the opportunity to better control their intellectual assets as opposed to (often mentioned in the literature) temporal and geographical limitations of IPR.

Readers also get an insight into whether or not IPR management and IP management are one and the same and if this really matters. Numerous plate sections containing quotes of IPR experts enrich this chapter.

5.1   WHAT'S SO SPECIAL ABOUT IPRS? AN IP EXECUTIVE'S VIEW

When top IP executives speak of IPM or IPRM, they are mostly referring to intellectual property rights themselves, especially patents and not to the management thereof. Figure 5.1 demonstrates the results of interviews as they point this out even though interviewees were not specifically asked about IPR.

Furthermore, respondents mentioned patents in as much as 15% of all coded segments of interviews. This is important to keep in mind as you

Fig. 5.1   Incident of used terms (interviews timeline)

read through the following section, as our respondents manage the intellectual property in IPR savvy companies. Nonetheless, this puts them in the position to gather ample knowledge of how to handle IPR issues, which is also valuable for those who are just starting out in the area.

Figure 5.2 shows, most notably, respondents' focus on the fact that IPRs are business assets. When asked to differentiate between IPR and other intangibles, their answers can be structured into two categories: those related to the business view and those related to the administrative view.

Interestingly, the distinction of temporal and geographical limitations between IPR and other forms of intangibles, which is often put forward in the literature, is mentioned less often. The same can be said for the

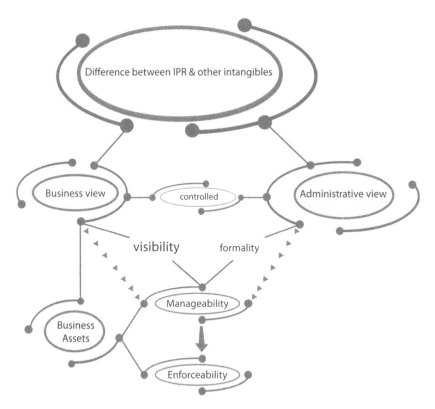

Fig. 5.2 Difference between IPR and other intangibles

provisions of the patent system forcing applicants to reveal parts of their invention, which is often mentioned by SMEs (indeed, this is also indicated in our interviews with people in charge of managing the IPR in smaller companies). Respondents do mention lengthy procedures, which is also one of the reasons the development and IPR processes are parallel (and there is a need for stage-gates as we note later on).

What is mostly put at the forefront are the manageability and the opportunity to better control the company's intellectual assets. Respondents focus on the fact that inventions embodied in IPR and the activities surrounding them are well described. This not only allows for the control of the commercialization of intellectual property but also for easier control of internal processes related to IPR.

> We struggle with trade secrets, because companies usually find it difficult to manage trade secrets and maintain records related to them. We are starting to build the system ourselves, but it is something that IP departments often do not track. /.../ I have recently been involved in some major transactions. When the purchaser asks you if you can list all your trade secrets, it is very difficult to provide the answer. They often use SOP and documents held by the business, that the IP department never sees.
>   Head of Legal Operations and IP Management,
>   European multinational pharmaceutical company
>
> Through the registration process you can attest the dates, facts, which makes the statutory protected rights more tangible than the non-registered rights.
>   Corporate Patent Manager,
>   Belgian multinational chemical company

The latter is also due to the ease of constructing a timeline, which is an important feature in various situations (such as in IP-related tax issues, IPR enforcement processes, etc.). The formalization of the IPR process is hence also highly detailed.

> Registered rights require a higher degree of formalisation—well described, with a timestamp and therefore easier to manage. /.../When talking to tax officers on transfer price issues or with development partners regarding background IP, patents are always quicker and easier to list than non-formalised know-how. /.../E.g. in a certain country you have established a subsidiary two years ago; and for the license agreement to the subsidiary, a 5% license fee on the sales needs to be paid. Upon being questioned by the local tax office you now need to attach

a date and additional information to the technology; and that is the moment of truth. For the non-formalised know-how you can have difficulties describing what is actually being transferred. Whereas with a patent this is much easier.
Chief IP Counsel,
German international automotive supplier

Most notably IP executives focus on long-term management of IPR and do so with a view at their whole IP portfolios. IPRs are seen as business assets, whose maintenance is expensive. This requires their efficient management.

A higher degree of manageability and through this increased enforceability (as they are more readily enforceable)—especially when using IPR offensively—is the route through which IPR management will achieve its goals and IPR costs become justified. Also, what is often seen as a high degree of formality in IPR processes and is hence regarded as a negative feature of so-called formalized or statutorily protected (sometimes called registered rights) can on the other hand be harvested in positive ways, as it also allows for higher control of and more structured processes.

5.2   Is IPR Management Simply IP Management?

There is a general conception that there is either no distinction between the two or one is a subset of the other. This is often affirmed by both the fact that we usually speak only of the IP departments and that IPR and other intangibles are closely connected.

People sometimes speak about IP management even if they mean IPR management. /.../ In the end it turns out that 99% of IPR management in my case is relating to patents, trademarks and design.
Chief IP Counsel,
German international automotive supplier

Looking from the organizational perspective, IP management is traditionally (and sometimes in less IPR savvy companies still) often handled by the R&D department/people, whereas dealing with IPR would often be the work of the legal department. In companies with structured IP departments, the roles merge to a certain degree, nonetheless looking more in depth we can see they deal primarily with IPR. We have affirmed the above-mentioned also in the previous subchapter as IP managers of IPR savvy companies mostly see their work as managing IPR and, to a lesser degree, other non-formalized forms of IP. Why then today are they mostly called IP departments? Historically, one of our interviewees company's IP department goes even back to the end-nineteenth century (under the name patent department), but a lot of them were established in the early, mid-, and late twentieth century—for example, the leading patent applicant in the world, IBM, established the patent department in 1926 (IBM 2017), reshaped it later to be the IP Law Department (Ma 2008; IBM 2017). The IP department is now the predominant designation. As one of our respondents pointed out a bit humorously:

> *Generally, it is IP department. /.../I think the reason for this is because the creation of the term IP department or IP management was done before anybody really knew what management of intellectual property rights really meant and what parts of management were affected. So, they just called themselves the IP department.*
> *Ex-Chief Trademark Counsel,*
> *German multinational automotive corporation*

Humour aside, the above arguments are strongly in favour of a notion that IP management and IPR management are one and the same or even more so that IPR management is a subset of IP management. Nonetheless, in the continuation we try to delve deeper into some of the differences between them.

The scope seems to be somewhat different for IPM and IPRM (see Fig. 5.3). The focuses of IPRM are IPR and their management. Hence, defining and utilizing IPR assets stands at the forefront of IPRM activities. This goes for both creating them and their commercialization. The goal is to secure the legal right to use and exploit the invention as well as to limit the exploitation of the underlying invention by others without payment— also by enforcing these rights before the courts (or via non-judicial paths).

The goal of IPRM is to effectively create added value of the IPR, which is valued on one hand explicitly by measuring the financial value of the IPR (either related to the end-product price or the price of leasing or selling the IP) and on the other non-explicitly (or in a more hidden manner) by securing their owner's competitive advantage. To be able to measure the latter, the competitive environment often needs to be analysed as a part of IPR processes. The non-formalized or non-statutory (also sometimes referred to as non-registered) mechanisms of protection are a

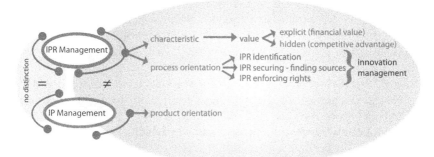

Fig. 5.3   Are IPR management and IP management one and the same?

complement to the intellectual property rights and do not stand in the forefront on their own.

IPRM is strongly process oriented. As we will touch upon later, IPR processes are very formalized. This is true for both the management of internal relationships and interactions with the outside (especially so, when dealing with governmental agencies). The latter strongly influences the internal relationships and processes—as compliance with these outside prerequisites needs to be reached—and consequently influences the efficiency of those processes. Though IPR processes generally begin and end within the organization, it is the interactions with the outside (e.g. government agencies) that greatly influence the creation or extension of bottlenecks, resource overlap, greater idle times, and so on within the organization. These characteristics are used as a measurement tool to evaluate and re-evaluate the process-oriented activities and are all based on the interactions with the outside.

Trade secrets or know-how on their own is generally not of interest to the companies. They only focus on one or the other if they are related to companies' already existing strategic or commercial interests. This brings us to the fact that IPM processes are strongly connected to product development and indeed many times IPR experts noted that IP processes are an auxiliary to product development processes (for more on this, see the next segment on IPR management as a business process). Linking IPM processes to product development and as such defining them as auxiliary processes means that intellectual property plays a key role in activities such as discovery, scoping, building business case, development, and testing as well as product launch and post-launch reviewing. Defining the IP process as an auxiliary process and consequently the just-mentioned activities also means their main function is supporting the execution of the IPR process (and all its sub-processes). The work of IPRM just barely begins within the time scope of research and product development, although it is strongly intertwined with it (consult the segment on integrated IPRM).

Our next question to the executives dealt with the formalization of IPRM processes as this is a distinctive feature of these processes. Consequently, we were also interested in whether the formalization could bring about the optimization of IPR processes. In other words: what is the added value of formalizing IPR processes?

The results clearly show the prevalence of positive attitudes towards formalization (see Fig. 5.4). This might be surprising at a first glance, as many theorists and practitioners warn against the formalization of all processes connected to innovation. However, as we will see in the continuation, this is not the case with IPR process formalization. A caveat is needed here; as top IP officers' tasks are often connected not only with individual

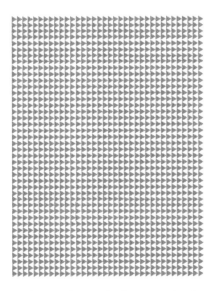

Fig. 5.4 Positive and negative attitude towards formalization. Legend: green = positive attribution; red = negative attribution

processes (e.g. patent application) but also encompass organizational and strategic perspectives (e.g. ensuring harmonized patent processes), we believe them to be more inclined towards a positive attitude than, for example, the employees in the research department.

Resistance is futile, you will be assimilated. In other words, although the first impression would be that formalization hinders the optimization of IPR processes, this is not the case at all. Why?

> *If there is somewhere in the company where the processes need to be formalized, it is intellectual property. If you make a formal mistake, your intellectual property rights will be gone. This is different to usual business, where a formal mistake mostly does not create the destruction of your asset.*
>   Chief Intellectual Property Officer,
>   European telecommunications company

Due to IPR's formal nature, their management demands a certain degree of formalization. Looking from the perspective of process management, formalization actually enables process automatization (through computerization of activities). Only then the identification of any bottlenecks can occur efficiently. Consequently, the company is able to start considering process optimization by removing or reducing the effects of bottlenecks that were identified.

Figure 5.5 presents the characteristics influencing the formalization of IPR processes. The latter is strongly linked to the monitoring activities as well as ensuring that no as little as possible bottlenecks exist or are dealt with efficiently. Monitoring activities are also influenced by the outside formalization demands, whereas the smoothness of the IPR process is influenced by the potential integration of IPR issues into the innovation and development processes. Both are used to prevent any information loss as well as to ensure that any required actions are done on time. The more formalized the IPR process, the smoother the IPR process is, and the number of bottlenecks (errors) is decreased to a minimum. What can formalization contribute in order to optimize a process? As mentioned before, formalization can be seen as the predecessor and a necessary step for the company to start thinking about the optimization of its processes. Both are clearly linked through a process of automatization, effective process execution, as well as monitoring. The latter is definitely an important aspect because not only are IPR seen as assets, but they also need to meet outside demands (of the legal and administrative systems) for formaliza-

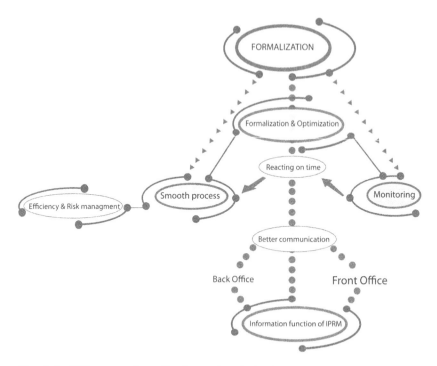

Fig. 5.5 IPR process formalization and optimization

tion. However, having formalized IPR processes, the company does not by default have optimized processes as well. Better communication is crucial and a link to the activities carried out in the Back-office. Generally, it is not always true that only formalized IPR processes can also be effective processes, but having formalized processes can make establishing optimized IPR processes a much easier task to manage.

In this subchapter we compare the terms IP management and IPR management. We find two streams: one not seeing any difference and the other in practice realizing IPR management has a somewhat different focus. *Nonetheless, we point out that IPRM and IPM need to be aligned with the overall commercial strategy of the company. This is something one needs to keep in mind, regardless of speaking (or focusing on) about either one.* The second part of this subchapter deals with formalization of IPR processes—as this is a strongly formalized process. This formalization has several consequences; we try to focus on the positive ones as these are in the literature less often pointed out. Part of Chap. 7 also discusses IPR tools supporting these processes in general as well as their formalization.

5.3   SHOULD YOU HANDLE YOUR IPR PROCESSES AS BUSINESS PROCESSES AND WHY (NOT)?

Figure 5.6 shows that IP executives expressed a positive view of IPRM processes being like any other business processes. They believe that in relation to B2B customers, IPRM processes provide various benefits for the company. Additionally, they also support internal stakeholders. Business partners (B2B customers) recognize the potential value of the output through the umbrella protection, as well as improved franchise recognition. They however struggle to recognize the value for the consumers (in B2C relationships). Some see the value as directly related to the quality and standard assurance.

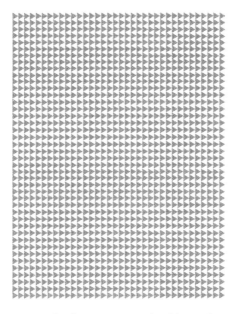

Fig. 5.6   IPR processes as business processes (positive and negative attribution). Legend: green = positive attribution; red = negative attribution

Fig 5.7   IPR process as business process

Figure 5.7 shows the attribution of value to all the above-mentioned categories. At this point it is important to understand the term "customer" as broadly as possible, meaning that a customer is any stakeholder that is in some way influenced by the output and is able to value the output based on said influence.

Let us concentrate on the value for the business, as there are many ways IPR process can create value for the business. Securing the possibility to appropriate (maximum) gains from development processes being just one way.

We want to point out two additional outputs that are generating value beyond direct customers (although we still consider them "value for the business" as in the end they serve the overall company's' strategy): the first one is the donation of IPR as the donation of IPR within the pharmaceutical pools is often mentioned. There is also the trend of opening the access to the IPR of some big companies such as Tesla, Toyota, LG Group, and so on, which is either done on a broad basis or to certain research entities (e.g. Fujitsu). The value generated is that of positive signalling, new market creation, or potential further out-licensing (of more core technologies, etc.). The second one also stems from the "hoarding" of IPR by big IPR savvy multinationals but regards creating value for society by matchmaking and simultaneously creating new services for third parties by IPR departments (often separated in affiliated companies)—redesigning to a degree their own business models by including services that do not rely only on managing the IPR portfolio of the company itself. Consider the case study in Box 5.1 as a case-in-point.

The interviewees were asked about the innovation potential of IPR management. They described three views of the innovation potential of IPR management, which we can see as value for internal stakeholders as seen from Fig. 5.8.

Box 5.1 The case of Panasonic IP matchmaking efforts
Panasonic has, like many others, amassed a considerable IPR portfolio. Like some other companies and following the change in the Japanese Trust Law, in 2014 Panasonic had set up a separate company—the Panasonic Intellectual Property Management, Co., Ltd. (PIPM). PIPM manages and consolidates IP activities in Panasonic Group, as well as performs IP-connected analytics. It hence controls Panasonic's IP activities, that is, creation, protection, and utilization of Panasonic's IPR. Another thing to consider is Panasonic's strategy to go beyond their B2C orientation and focus more on B2B. The story does not end there. Realizing the unused potential of IPR, monetizing their huge IPR know-how and good knowledge of the IPR landscape, allows PIPM to think beyond the usual scope of IPR activities in IP departments. The plan: To introduce a new service into the IP(R) matchmaking market, connecting IPR creators and users. The matchmaking market in the IP field has so far been populated with university spin-off ventures and various consulting services companies or groups. However, PIPM can, due to its skills, knowledge, networks, reputation, and tradition, be in a good position to create a new stand-alone value creating output for Panasonic.

Panasonic thus views its IPR as value-creating assets, rather than simply legal rights. PIPM also became responsible for its own performance and achieving revenue targets. This in turn creates a powerful incentive for monetizing relevant (especially non-core) portions of the Panasonic's IPR portfolio.

Sources:
Panasonic. (2017). *PIPM promotion pamphlet*. Osaka: Panasonic.
Ellis, J. (2015). Panasonic makes its case as Japan's IP strategy leader with royalty-free and open source plans. *IAM Magazine*. Retrieved from http://www.iam-media.com/blog/detail.aspx?g=4977355a-7b77-4b80-b4f7-ba6760386d03
Pasona Knowledge Partner webpage. Retrieved from https://pasona-kp.co.jp/
Panasonic. (2014). 知的財産業務を集約・事業化する新会社を10月より本格稼働:プレスリリース/Full-scale operation of new company that intensifies and commercializes intellectual property business from October: News release. Retrieved from http://news.panasonic.com/jp/press/data/2014/09/jn140922-2/jn140922-2.html

Firstly, the respondents point out the informational value as IPR and IPRM demand clear (and codified) information, from defining valuable inventions and IP assets to FTO analysis (describing the external environment of the invention at hand). Trade secrets may be the mechanism of choice for protection, yet their manageability is problematic even in bigger, more IP savvy companies (this was also pointed out by our interviewees). This is sometimes detrimental to companies' abilities to really cash in on their IP assets. Also, especially for smaller companies, the signalling function via acquired patents in a certain field can strengthened their position and be seen as more desirable in terms of cooperation partners—so the business potential is also pointed out.

Secondly, it fosters an innovative climate, as it demands better communication in terms of innovation activities inside the company as well as communication on the utilization of innovation. This better communication also helps nurture a standardized IPR process, which can help close gaps and inefficiencies caused by differentiated IPR processes and streamline the IPR activities, helping the involved staff to perform more efficiently. Furthermore, it makes the participation in the creation of the innovation transparent, with the potential to increase the motivation to invent.

> *People are given credit for the innovation they did. So that might help to foster an innovation climate in the company. People are proud to contribute—and if you contribute, you are seen.*
>   *Chief IP Counsel,*
>   *German international automotive supplier*

Thirdly, IPR management helps generalizing ideas by defining a broader scope of the applicability of the innovation and consequently broadening the scope of IP rights—thus in turn allowing for higher potential from a certain IP right. This enables not only the safe utilization of the invention at hand but also many times the applicability of the IPR to at least some future improvements as well as the use of the invention for other purposes as originally designed (in some other process, as a part of another product, etc. or even via another way of monetizing the invention at hand—e.g. via out-licensing).

> *IP staff is in a position to generalize ideas and make sure that they become protected by broad IP rights. This is also an additional value to innovation,*

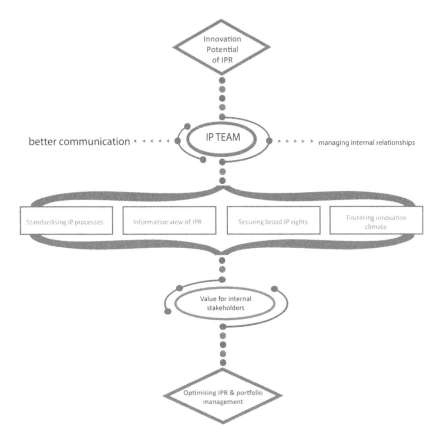

Fig. 5.8   Innovation potential of IPR management

which can only be realised with the participation of an experienced patent attorney. E.g. in many cases, the aspects that end up protected by IP rights, are not one and the same as the inventors initial idea.
   Senior Vice-President, Chief IP Counsel,
   German conglomerate manufacturing and electronics company

Interestingly, when asked about the innovation potential of IPRM, top IP executives frequently focused on internal gains although they do acknowledge its business value. Benefits especially in terms of optimized IPRM processes, more fluency in activities, and interim outputs are pointed out.

Figure 5.9 shows different sub-processes of IPRM, through which IPRM potential can be realized and (interim) outputs are achieved. Furthermore, we show the interplay with the development process. *Top IP executives know how to recognize value in different segments; they take a holistic view, where the value for the company is seen both in external value and the value extracted from their providing support to internal stakeholders through various interim outputs. The latter is not to be considered negligible as it straightens the intellectual property itself and enables the information function of the IPR management.*

Our respondents agree that stage-gates inside both IPRM and especially the development processes are very common. As mentioned in Chap. 3, their goal is to ensure relevant considerations are made at specific points in order to propel the process forward (or not). They are also called "toll gates" or "quality gates" or "decision gates" and are seen sometimes as a "continuous exercise." Our sub-processes correspond to the stages in the stage-gate models, and the gates would correspond to the points where both processes interplay (see also the part on integrated IPRM processes).

> *There are several so-called quality gates. That is a common term in the engineering world and we have adapted this to our /IPRM/ processes as well. So that within /.../ quality gates we can capture quality gaps/.../ so our own input /..../ fills the quality gate for decision-making.*
>   *Ex-Chief Trademark Counsel,*
>   *German multinational automotive corporation*

Due to the complexity of the IPRM sub-processes themselves, we will not be able to address the issue more in depth later on (and we do not show the parallel development process activities). However, we describe briefly their interplay here.

> *The core /R&D/ process is, a toll-gate process, a milestone driven activity, to get investment allowance for the next research step /.../ to have a sustainable result from the R&D efforts. The activities of this core process are interacting with the IPR stream. It is advantageous if the same people decide on either to file a patent or not and to continue with the product project or not etc. It also means interacting people-wise, since stakeholders cross-participate, in order that investment decisions are done with the knowledge of IP in mind.*
>   *Chief IP Counsel,*
>   *German international automotive supplier*

Fig 5.9 IPR and development processes through stage-gate model lens. Source: Development cycle based on Cooper (1988)

Looking at the development stages (or sub-processes), we see they start with the discovery, which is in its essence an intellectual exercise and was not included in the original model by Cooper (1988). Thus, these are not separate processes per se as both encompass the same activities. IPR pre-evaluation is roughly parallel to scoping and building the business case, and IPR activities on several points produce not only results to determine whether to push the IPR forward or not but also to help determine if pushing the product along the development pipeline is the correct business decision and henceforth to continue with the development process. Alkaersig et al. (2015) have shown some stage-gate considerations for companies divided into IP Dealers, IP Strategists, and IP Rookies, focusing especially for stages until the launch.

> *In the middle of the development project is a critical decision point. You have to decide whether you will industrialize a certain technical concept. Some critical issues are: Do you run into third party IP that makes the investment impossible to realize? Is it a product that is so unique on the market that it can be patent protected, so that you can ask for higher margins for it, because the patent could cause less competition around its features? There is a natural point in the life of a project when you need to make that assessment. That is critical. If you get it wrong, there might be severe consequences. There is a risk and an opportunity at that point of time. Being involved in that decision is important to the IP department despite all the uncertainties.*
> *Chief IP Counsel,*
> *German international automotive supplier*

In the last gate, before the launch stage, Alkaersig et al. (2015) believe the following IP issues should be considered: aligning the IP strategy with the expected lifecycle of a product, planning IP enforcement and the identification of infringements, assigning a continuous budget for IP, and identifying stakeholders in charge of IP reassessments. Nonetheless, keep in mind that although our interviewees pointed out that the IPRM goes along with the product, the IPRM might continue even if the product will not be moved forward. Decisions on what course of action will be undertaken in terms of the IPR are still needed (kept for strategic reasons, exploitation on markets for ideas, etc.). Thus, the value of IPR is not only indirectly measured by the value/price of the product on the market but also the mere value of IPR even when the product never reaches the market. Also the post-launch reviews stage is in today's IPR landscape extremely important for the development stage as it allows the reaction to new or changed circumstances as well as improvement needs—together with the corresponding stages (sub-processes) of commercialization, enforcement, and post-evaluation. These are not static and do not stop to interact with the launch and cannot be seen as a static gate consideration before this stage, as Alkaersig et al. (2015) figures might imply. The lesson is that the interplay of the IPRM process with other (business) processes needs to be strong and consistent (please also consult the part on integrated process in Chap. 6).

We now focus on whether or not we can see IPRM as a business process. When identified as business processes, IPR processes focus on value-added outputs and do so regardless of the target audience. Such a view can prosper in a process-oriented organization. Many of the top IPR savvy companies, however, mainly consist of traditional structures. Consequently, two types of processes are identified—core and auxiliary. The first execute day-to-day operations, whereas the latter support the efficient execution of the first.

Below we can see why IPR executives deem IPR processes as auxiliary. Table 5.1 shows what IPR executives focus on when discussing this. Furthermore, we discern if—looking from organizational and business process management perspectives—it really matters whether the IPR process is identified as core or auxiliary?

There is a tendency in literature, as well as in practice, to think in terms of processes being "core" or "auxiliary." Even IP experts often suggest IPR processes be considered as auxiliary. Why? The short answer seems to be that IPRs are not (or should not) be a goal in itself.

You need to extract as much value as you can from that asset. There are two flows. One flow is when an intellectual property right as an asset is exploited on its own. On the other hand, you can use intellectual property right to enhance the other business of the company. In our company, we work with both flows.

Table 5.1 IPR process as a core or auxiliary process

Weight	Emphasis
0.25	Secondary in terms of focus
0.19	Auxiliary process for the product creation process
0.15	Common decision structure
0.09	Interaction with others
0.08	More formalized
0.04	Secondary in terms of budget allocation

Chief Intellectual Property Officer,
European telecommunications company

A longer answer encompasses the following (as outlined in Table 5.1):

1. For an active company (whose main activity is not trading IPR in any form), IPR processes are secondary in terms of focus—the focus being on other processes such as product development. The latter is also seen many times as the principal or core process for the IPR processes. Note however that IPR processes remain an important feature long after the product development stage has been completed.
2. The decision structure is ingrained in other processes as IPR are not a goal of their own, but need to be aligned with other processes in the company. This also brings with it the interaction with other stakeholders in the company (but outside the IP department).
3. Also, what seems to indicate IPR's more auxiliary nature is its high level of formalization, which is often associated with other processes and activities often seen as auxiliary as well (such as business administration).
4. Lastly, the budgeting focus should not lie primarily on the IPR acquisition, as other processes and activities will need to be accomplished first in order for IPR to be able to serve their primary function of allowing the appropriation of gains that can be enhanced through IPR.

Does it really matter if we could describe it as a core or as an auxiliary process? Our respondents believe it is a process managed in the background that has a very high impact. Let us point out again that in the literature, three types of processes can be identified: core, support, and management (Ould 1995) or core, support, and improvement (Kock and McQueen 1998). The first of these processes present the functioning of the company, the second are those processes the core processes cannot exist without, whereas the management/improvement processes deal with the efficient organization and execution of the two through knowledge exchange. A further distinction between the core and support (or auxiliary) processes can also be identified through the lens of the customer's type, as core processes focus on fulfilling external customers' needs, whereas the auxiliary processes focus on fulfilling the internal customers' needs (Ould 1995).

Going back to Fig. 5.9, it clearly presents the IPRM process linked with the development process. We cannot argue that the latter is either the management process (as according to Ould (1995)) or the improvement process (according to Kock and McQueen (1998)); however, both IPRM process and the development process together consist of the activities that contribute to the production of the value-added output for known customers. Focusing now on core and auxiliary (support) processes, the function of the latter is to support the successful implementation of the first (if no core processes are executed, the need for support processes becomes obsolete). Even though Ould (1995) defined one of the differences between the two as providing output for external or internal customers, one could argue that in the case of IPRM, this is not the case as the "type" of end-customer does not really influence the activities in the IPRM process itself.

Looking from the real-world application side, the distinction between IPR core and auxiliary is trivial as IPR executives' focus rather on execution and the IPR delivery. However, it is of key importance to provide some clearance in this rather complex field. We argue that IPR processes are in fact business processes. They have all the elements business process should have—they only start once the input has been identified, they consist of a set of linked parallel and/or consecutive activities (sometimes grouped in either work processes or sub-processes), their end result in an output has value for the customer. Again, we need to think of end-customer in a broad sense as possible, either external or internal, a physical consumer or a legal entity. Therefore, companies need to recognize IPR processes as business processes, handle them as such, try to eliminate any real or potential bottlenecks, and focus on effective (cost/time/quality) output delivery.

The aim of this chapter was to present the first part of the analysis of interviews with top IP(R) executives from some of the world's leading multinationals. The chapter investigates the difference between IPRs and other intangibles by comparing on one hand the administrative and business views and on the other hand trying to identify the differences in regard to the controlling, manageability, and enforceability. The chapter further investigated the difference between IP processes and IPR processes, firstly from the executive's perspective as well as from the process management perspective. *IPR processes are business processes, consisting of an input, linked activities, and producing an output. The quicker the companies recognize IPR processes as business processes, the quicker they could manage them efficiently, thus ensuring the delivery of a high added value output.* Finally, by digging in deeper, the chapter also presented why IPR processes are business processes and should consequently be handled as such. This enables the reader to continue on the path of managing IPR through the lenses of Back-office and Front-office, explored in Chap. 6.

REFERENCES

Alkaersig, L., Beukel, K., & Reichstein, T. (2015). *Intellectual property rights management: Rookies, dealers and strategists.* Hampshire: Palgrave.
Cooper, R. G. (1988). *Winning at new products.* London: Kogan Page.
IBM. (2017). Patents and innovation. Retrieved from http://www-03.ibm.com/ibm/history/ibm100/us/en/icons/patents/team/
Kock, N., & McQueen, R. J. (1998). An action research case-study of effects of asynchronous groupware support on productivity and outcome quality of process redesign groups. *Journal of Organizational Computing and Electronic Commerce, 8*(2), 149–168.
Ma, A. (2008). IBM, patent leadership: Balances proprietary and collaborative innovation. *China Intellectual Property*, Feb. 2008(22).
Ould, A. M. (1995). *Business process modelling and analysis for re-engineering and improvement.* New York: Wiley.

CHAPTER 6

IPR Characteristics in Practice: Back-Office to Front-Office

Abstract This chapter answers the question of IPRM characteristics and scope. First, we delve into attributes such as "integrated," "aligned," and so on to discern their meaning in practice in IPR savvy companies. We show what is behind these often used monikers.

Second, we present the strategic IPRM framework and then proceed with defining the scope of IPRM through the bundle of activities defined as Back-office, Front-office, or Mixed, extending upon the last part of Chap. 5. We show not only the complementarity of legal and administrative tasks with business-oriented tasks but also the broad involvement of different employees and different departments. We present a flowchart of IPR process activities. The chapter is enriched with citations by the top IP executives. We provide interview-based recommendations for successful IPR practices.

Keywords Characteristics of IPR management • Back-office • Front-office • IPRM organizational structures • Strategic level of IPR • IPR process flowchart • TAD methodology

In this chapter we start by focusing on the characteristics of IPRM, such as integrated, aligned, seamless, comprehensive, and outward looking. Most of the chapter is however dedicated to taking a more in-depth look into IPRM by focusing on its two dimensions: the Back-office and the Front-office, their scope, and links between them.

6.1   What Should IPRM Really Be Like? On the Characteristics of IPRM

When taking in the information about the attributes of IPRM, words like "integrated" and "aligned" appear quite often. What does that mean for some of the top IPR executives in practical terms?

The key point top IPR executives make is that IPR management should be integrated (see Fig. 6.1). But what should it be integrated with (as above we focus only on its interplay with development processes)?

> *Integrated would mean: align goals, have a common decision structure with core processes (i.e. R&D), have decision points within processes which bring up questions related to IPR.*
>
> Chief IP Counsel,
> German international automotive supplier

> */IPR processes/should always be integrated; the way you develop, secure and enforce IPR, needs to be aligned with the overall business strategy.*
>
> Head of Legal Operations and IP Management,
> European multinational pharmaceutical company

They see this integration as threefold. Firstly, there is the interaction between all key stakeholders of IPR processes (the HR aspect). Secondly, there is the need to integrate IPR processes with other processes in the

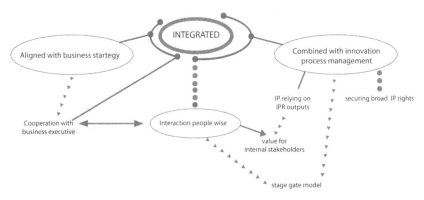

Fig. 6.1 Integrated

company (the process-oriented aspect), and thirdly, they point out the alignment with the overall business strategy (the business value aspect).

Interaction with a company's top executive officers is crucial when aligning IPR processes with the overall business strategy and operationalization thereof. This ensures that IPRs are being registered and maintained, which in turn helps the company generate enriched outputs. The integration with the product lifecycle management through the stage-gate model was already mentioned as well as a common decision structure with core processes—all the way from the early stage harvest.

> *In our company we have a general process for PLM—Product Lifecycle Management—and within this process different gates are defined, where in the end the R&D team has to deliver a certain product. The IP questions are included in those gates. That means each R&D team needs to have answers regarding IP rights issues. For example about freedom to operate searches at the very beginning, then about patent protection and in the later stages, the issues about IP portfolio management.*
>
> COO of the subsidiary IPR company,
> German conglomerate manufacturing and electronics company

The interim results valuable to internal stakeholders can be distributed to employees in all sub-processes (or in other words stages), which have a need for them. The IP is hence relying on the IPR output, helping to achieve the overall business strategy.

If IPR processes are integrated, do they influence other processes or do other processes influence them and how do these synergies come to be? The word seamless comes to mind often (Fig. 6.2).

> *One that comes to my mind is seamless; so that you don't hold up the processes. /.../Having the least impact in a negative way on R&D processes.*
>
> Chief IP Counsel,
> German international automotive supplier

> *We have to make sure that /.../ the business people do not feel disturbed; and that we achieve a good protection for the competitive advantage in a smooth and seamless way.*
>
> Senior Vice-President, Chief IP Counsel,
> German conglomerate manufacturing and electronics company

> *IPR, by definition, is something which creates disturbances as it creates exclusive domains. That is by definition. So, if IPR is seamless, then I think you don't exploit the IPR.*
>
> Chief Intellectual Property Officer,
> European telecommunications company

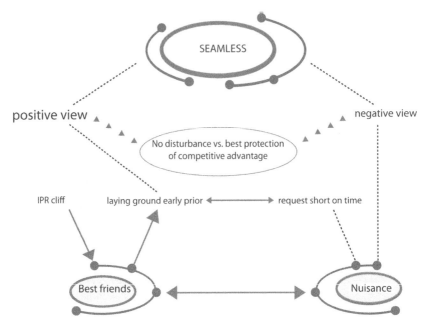

Fig. 6.2 Seamless

IPR processes' influence on other processes is twofold. On one hand there is a positive influence, when laying the foundation early on and/or when a situation of a so-called IPR cliff occurs (when external factors may put either the IPR or its utilization at risk). The emphasis here is on IPR processes providing support for other (core) processes and that interaction with other stakeholders is very important. Hence, establishing good communication channels within the company does not only ensure seamless IPR processes but also smooth core processes.

> *I would interpret this in a way where there is no disruption in the chain of management. So that there is no gap and results from one process flow seamlessly to the next process and create a new decision. That's my understanding of seamless.*
>
> Ex-Chief Trademark Counsel,
> German multinational automotive corporation

On the other hand, IPR processes are often not perceived as decreasing bottlenecks, but rather as being a nuisance (for other processes). Delays in research, research collaborations, as well as delays in publications are often mentioned. In this view, IPR process is simply a futile and expensive exercise. It seems this view prevails when requests to the IPR team are made on a (too) short notice, because the IPR team then struggles with creating their IPR interim output in due time.

> *I will give you an example of getting requests where there is not much time to react. Business people call us when preparing for a trade fair, where they want to present new technology. Suddenly there is necessity for a further filing beforehand. When requests that are very short on time happen, it is quite a challenge. However, when we have more time, we include our services quite seamlessly into all other processes.*
>
> COO *of the subsidiary IPR company,*
> *German multinational industrial conglomerate*

There is no easy answer as to whether by increasing seamlessness, the IPR process enriches other processes—that is, increase the efficiency by doing things right by executing activities within the process in the best possible manner with the least waste of time or effectiveness of other processes by doing the right things and as a consequence successfully contribute to the production of the desired outcome. Nonetheless, seamless IPRM represent an antecedent of our efforts for smooth process flow. A smooth process flow is characterized with less bottlenecks and gaps as well as errors. This includes instances when requests are made short on time, where IPRM with its activities present at least a minimal quality check in terms of innovativeness and the competitive IPR environment by, for example, decreasing possible problems after the launch of the product. Not only is lowering the number of bottlenecks, gaps, and errors important for seamless IPRM, it is also crucial for the firm to identify such potential "problems" as quickly as possible and respond to them within advance prepared scenarios.

There are—at least—two more features of IPR management. The first one is outward looking, the second is comprehensive (Fig. 6.3).

The outward-looking feature demonstrates itself threefold: *firstly*, through combining IPR principles with principles of open innovation. *Secondly*, the outward-looking feature is a part of many individual activities, from assessing detectability to clearance searches and prior art searches

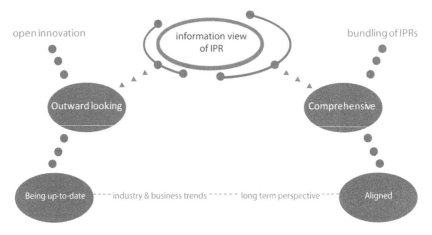

Fig. 6.3 Comprehensive and outward looking

and industry and business trend analysis. *Thirdly*, providing up-to-date context for your innovation and for the IPR, this is crucial. Hence, taking into account industry and business trends is valuable not only for immediate decision-making but also in the long-term perspective, ensuring alignment with other (business) processes (e.g. R&D processes, etc.). The informational function of IPRM comes to the forefront again.

How then is IPR management comprehensive? Its comprehensive nature is clear in, for example, the bundling of IPR rights, determining the geographical scope of IPR protection that is sought, as well as in taking into account alignment with product strategy. Also, our respondents again mention product-by-product base, comprehensive processes being achieved through alignment with others, especially product development processes.

6.2   Strategic IPRM

The strategic function of the IPRM is extremely important and frames the individual process flows we describe in the next section (as well as the use of the IPR TAD tool we present further on). The larger the operation, the more important this level of IPRM is—nonetheless, the principles of strategic IPRM should be taken into account by large as well as small companies: both when they think about re-organizing their IPR process as well as inside individual (operational level) process flows.

I have a slightly different spin here, because I work for a very large corporation which has more than 50 thousand patents applications and patents, and around 80 thousand trademarks. So my role and function as the head of the IP management are different to those of the people in the division IP departments and their heads.

When they talk about managing IPR they e.g. talk about identifying IPR, finding sources to secure IPR, enforcing IP rights and making sure their IPR is aligned with the commercial strategy around their products. That's IPRM in the traditional sense. However, in a big business' perspective you also need to create the framework and create IPRM principles, plan the structure of the IPR ownership in the company—e. g. how to deal with the transfer of licenses between individual companies inside the group, how to transfer rights in and out of the company or companies through deals. Another aspect is looking at the risk management. Are there practices within the company that can potentially undermine our rights, or are there things we need to bring in to strengthen those rights? Finally, you also need to deal with whether or not there are underused IPR in the company and if we can get value for these rights by out-licensing them.

However, while doing this, you are not dealing with the specifics. It is more process orientated. So there is quite a different role to what an average IP department does which is more product focused.

Head of Legal Operations and IP Management,
European multinational pharmaceutical company

Although the theory will give us the impression that IPR strategy is preceding the IPRM activities on the operational level, the usual evolution of a more coherent IPR strategy does not really follow this theoretical presumption. Still, to simplify the strategic IPRM, we will go through Fig. 6.4 "as-if" this would be true and begin our explanations with tasks or parts of IPR strategy (note, here only the parts that were especially pointed out by our respondents are put forward—for a more coherent overview, see Chap. 2).

Firstly, defining goals is of utmost importance. The goals can be connected with finding answers to the following two questions: "Are we using our resources wisely?" and "Is the business protected?," hence answering the question on IPR efficiency and IPR effectiveness. Hence, the goals are connected to how the company utilizes and exploits its IPR: offensively, defensively, strategically, or as a signal of its R&D activities, on the IPR markets, as possible cooperation sign-points, and so on.

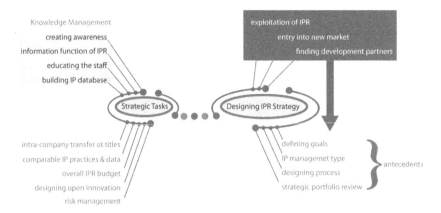

Fig. 6.4   Strategic IPRM

Some specific uses could also sometimes be discovered as we can see from the example below—nonetheless, this can have less to do with a coherent overall IPR strategy than with an ad hoc decision. Still, the awareness of different options to reach different (business) goals with the IPR is important.

> We once secured a market entry in a certain business segment for our business with our intellectual property. This certain business segment was blocked but we were able to open the entry into it. /…/We also used our intellectual property rights to buyout the shares of a minority shareholder in our company.
>
> Chief Intellectual Property Officer,
> European telecommunications company

Secondly, the decision on the IPR management type needs to be made. This has two dimensions: the managerial style (centralized or decentralized) and the organizational form (inside department, establishing own department outside IPRM company or relying on outside resources). Furthermore, the organizational format can be different from firm to firm. Our respondents come from both firms that have internal IP departments and those that have established their own individual business units (companies), who took over the management of the IPR for the group. Consider the below three models of IPRM organization.

The first one marks a fragmented organizational structure with IPR being managed on the level of business units (rarely, but still there are some organizations that have lowered it to the level of individual legal

FRAGMENT   CENTRALIZED   OUTSIDE

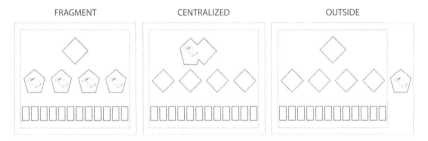

Fig. 6.5 IPRM organizational structures

entities)—depicted by the mid-level pentagons in Fig. 6.5. The middle picture depicts a centralized internal unit that is usually connected to the headquarters—in the picture the upper-level pentagon is attached to the headquarters quadrant. Establishing an individual business unit which manages the IPR for the group is very popular, especially in recent years. The depiction of this situation is on the right-hand side of Fig. 6.5 with the pentagon being outside the main business structure of different (usually product) business areas and their units and also outside the headquarters.

> *Our group, that in general has a long IP history, consists of approximately 500 single companies. We filed our first patent about 160 years ago and we have had an IP department for about 120 years. However, there was no central IP department until about 4 years ago, which is very different from some other big companies. At that time the new IP department became a central department for the whole group of companies, delivering IP related services to all of them. First we have been the department within the main company, but two years later a separate company was established. The same group of people that worked before in the centralized IP department now work here. To remain precise; we deliver IP related services, but the IP rights still belong to the legal entity.*
> *COO of the subsidiary IPR company,*
> *German multinational industrial conglomerate*

Usually this re-organization (via centralized IP functional units) goes hand in hand with the centralization of IPR-related activities, trying to achieve benefits from unified IPR processes.

> *One thing was the effectiveness of IP decisions by having homogenous processes. In recent years, before we had a centralized patent department, we've seen that some of our businesses already did a good job, but in other legal entities, we've*

seen that actually an IP-awareness did not even exist at all. The idea of central-izing was to establish homogeneous processes for the whole company. That means getting all legal entities on a high decision level for effective IP decisions.

COO of the subsidiary IPR company,
German multinational industrial conglomerate

The establishment of independent IP subsidiary can also affect the design of additional goals for IPRM, which are especially connected to generating financial income from IPRM. This can have both positive and negative effects. Positive if we consider the fact that sleeping patents and other IPR will be looked into if some benefits can be generated from these non-active IPRs. Negative if we believe that the IPRM could be guided solely to generate income—even at the expense of other (strategic) goals of the company or the group as a whole. Another topic connected to this is the centralization of IPR processes, trying to gain a harmonized and thus more efficient handling of IPR and prevent differentiated activities leading to diverse results, which can in turn have harmful effects in the long run.

One of the biggest issues is variation within the company. /.../ For example, a division, despite a change in US patent law, wanted to continue to name the inventors as applicants in the US. Another division has altered its practice to take advantage of the change in the law and they filed in the name of [company name]. From a management perspective this divergence of practice is undesir-able—especially when there might be legal consequences. So harmonization would be best, but it is a challenge for big companies with semi-autonomous units.

Head of Legal Operations and IP Management,
European multinational pharmaceutical company

This dimension also includes the decision of what role the IP(R) depart-ment will play in relation to other departments and the achievement of overall goals, where the IPR department is more or less included in the planning of overall long-term strategic and research goals.

Thirdly, the strategical part must be operationalized by activities done inside the IPR process. One of the mechanisms to achieve this is through strategic portfolio review. Or in other words, pruning is the operational outlet for keeping the IPR portfolio in line with the strategic goals.

In regular intervals we have workshops together with our business units to go through our whole patent stock; to see whether IPR is still core and/or if some detectability parameter has changed. That means we link the overall business strategy, our R&D strategy with the IP strategy. Within the workshops we question if a certain patent is still as important for our business as it was five years ago. Additionally, we have the IP dialogue as an annual meeting, where we link the R&D strategy with the IP strategy by defining IP focus topics and where we go through the whole patent stock.

/.../

We have the IP dialogue as an annual meeting to have a general discussion about R&D and IP strategy to define IP focus topics, but within the space of two years, we conduct a workshop where we go through the whole patent stock.

COO of the subsidiary IPR company,
German multinational industrial conglomerate

Why is it necessary? The idea is to be able to not waste resources on unimportant IPR (i.e. non-core IPR, which cannot be utilized inside any of the strategies: defensive, offensive, or leveraging—for more on them, please consult Chap. 2). Our interviewees believe this can also allow to gear the IPR process towards being lean (consult also the citation below). The issue of being lean is however also connected to another function of strategic IPRM: IPR budget planning.

Being lean on a small budget: First you make a risk assessment for a certain industry, whether from history or comparative analysis and see if IPR have helped gain an edge or on the other hand if third party IPR has caused a lot of damage. So you have a certain lever with IPR towards a competitive edge. Taking this into account, you would take a higher or smaller percentage (perhaps 1 or 2%) of the R&D budget for IP support. Hence you have a fixed amount of money to do your job. That is what it means to be lean, but not on account of missing any IPR related opportunities. This means it needs to be enough to e.g. allow us to have enough in-house people to review all projects; to see if our projects are not at risk due to third party IPR; or to see how many patents we can really file based on that money and in how many countries. The other element of being lean is how quickly you make decisions—how many meetings do you need before you can make that decision; and here you can be either extremely comprehensive, complex, hence slow, or you can be lean. That depends on how good you can communicate and relate to people.

Chief IP Counsel,
German international automotive supplier

Before moving on to IP knowledge management, we need to mention two more functions. The first is inherent of IPRM in big companies: the intra-company transfer of titles. This is many times strongly connected with business considerations (also those going beyond the question of which business unit could utilize the connected IP on the goods' market, but also exploit the IPR in other ways, or also dependent on other (external) factors—such as taxation issues). The second is risk management as a specific part of IPRM. There is a whole spectrum of activities connected to IPR risk management—aimed at ensuring optimal IPRM outputs. To start with checking IPR requirements or also known patents as the patentability search focuses mainly on novelty. One thing we need to keep in mind is that in the field of IPR there are hardly any one-to-one relationships. Here, the invention may not be described or incorporated in a single document—it suffices that later on the novelty could be compromised in the eyes of the examiner. Here anything that could be considered as prior art is included irrelevant of its form and (if dealing with another patent application) irrelevant of its validity. The next activity, which goes more in depth, is the prior arts search conducted primarily by the patent attorney sometimes assisted by the patent engineer. The full clearance search differs from this as its goal is to determine whether a particular product, service, or group of products or services, if commercialized, would infringe patents owned by others (i.e. does the company have the freedom to operate regarding the invention at hand when implemented in or applied as a certain product or service). Hence, only those presently active are taken into account. In terms of patents, the claims are closely examined—on the other hand, patent applications are not relevant per se, but only when there is a good chance of them transforming into active patents. As these are usually time consuming and costly, the need for a full clearance search comes when the decision to commercialize will be made (note there is another decision that is vastly dependent on this one: the decision to actively use the granted patent—which we could describe as an automatic milestone more or less). On the other hand, it can be costly to not conduct the full clearance search together with the invalidity search at the right time, as it can feed the R&D process, the commercialization process, as well as the IPR registration. Lastly, an invalidity analysis seeks to determine whether the patent office made a mistake and granted the patent owner more protection that they had a right to in view of the prior art (e.g. previous inventions and publications). In other words, an invalidity analysis asks: did the patent office grant the patent owner protection over an idea that is not new? An invalidity analysis requires further searching or consideration of the prior art to determine whether claimed features in the patent are in fact not new in view of that prior art. In the next subchapter, you can see how these elements are positioned throughout the individual IPR process.

One of our interviewees pointed out the contribution of scenario thinking as a way to engage in foresight and to mitigate (future) risks (as you will see in the next section, there are many activities that can help put together the puzzle of diminishing uncertainties). The lesson is to be able to see what is developed in the industry or sector, to be able to value your own IPR. As we mentioned the idea is to be able to predict contingencies for multiple possible future results and thereby rather than treat uncertainties as a crippling obstacle, the uncertainties are deliberated upon beforehand and ways to diminish the effects of a non-favourable events or IP or R&D environment changes (with the latter already being in the domain of contingency planning).

> When you do business, you have to think about the future and you have to think how you position yourself in the market, also with the help of IPR. One tool /.../ is scenario thinking. Making projections of what can happen in the future and seeing how you can position yourself.
>
> Chief Intellectual Property Officer,
> European telecommunications company

As discussed in Chap. 3, two of the three (overlapping) sub-processes that can be defined inside the innovation process can be applied to the IPR process as well: the production of knowledge and the matching of the artefacts to market needs and demands (Pavitt 2006). Knowledge management is a functional group of tasks inside the strategic IPRM. In order to do this, internal and external knowledge sources can be utilized. The first one is a manifestation of the open innovation paradigm. It can be utilized on various levels; as an example other companies' practices can be observed, analysed, and adapted into a company's own practices. The other one is in utilizing external sources of innovation (there is an extensive literature on this lately—e.g. Gassmann and Bader 2017).

> There is a syndrome called "Not Invented Here". If you believe that all the innovations and good ideas can only be created internally, then you will miss a big part of innovation, i.e. open innovation. Therefore, IPR management must also cover all open innovation aspects. Meaning collaboration with universities, collaboration with research institutes etc.
>
> Senior Vice-President, Chief IP Counsel,
> German conglomerate manufacturing and electronics company

We have already elaborated to some degree on the topic of the information function of the IPR and building awareness. In Sect. 7.2 we will also discuss the training and IPR education of the staff (both IPR staff and employees of other departments). A tangible result of the IPR knowledge management is also the IP database (for more see also Sect. 7.2).

6.3   Towards the Scope of IPRM
Through the Bundle of Back- and Front-Office Activities A.K.A. What Are We Really Doing?

Managing intellectual property rights has two dimensions: the legal-administrative dimension and the business dimension. Hence, IPR management means managing the so-called Back-office activities dealing with the legal and administrative dimension and Front-office activities finding how IPR can benefit the company. The Back-office could also be termed a technical aspect of IPR process management. Some would even call it the old-fashioned view of IPR process management.

> *You have to divide it into legal administrative processes and business processes and we have both.*
>
> Head of Legal Operations and IP Management,
> European multinational pharmaceutical company

The Back-office is most of all concerned with so-called preparation phase or the creation of IPR assets—from identifying valuable inventions by cooperating with the R&D department to defining the scope of the IPR (whereby including the co-creation of innovations). It is often influenced by external factors such as legal regulations and administrative procedures. The Back-office however reaches beyond this, offering support in evaluation and renewal processes and IPR enforcement issues. In short, it concerns itself with creating value and outputs for internal stakeholders. The Back-office thus strongly supports the informational function of IPR management, also providing inputs for other business processes.

The Front-office takes over where Back-office's function ends. Creating value for the business (company) is at the core of Front-office's activities. It concerns itself with co-creating a competitive advantage for the business and optimizing the handling of individual elements and the overall IPR portfolio. Its task is to provide support to the upper and top management. It requires to have not only a strong insight into its own processes but also to incorporate the knowledge about what the competitors are doing. In other words, the Front-office concerns itself with valuing and strategizing in order to maximize the benefits of IPR to the business.

The Front-office and Back-office together form what we call IPR management. By looking at this more in depth, three types of activities are defined:

1. Pure Back-office activities: these are purely administrative and legal activities—often strongly influenced by external pressures/influences/demands. Back-office activities are always undertaken as a response to a pressure/influence/demand from outside the Back-office. Even though the Back-office's activities are necessary, they individually do not add value to the IPR.
2. Pure Front-office activities: these activities are designed in a way to enable the maximization of IPR's added value. They are highly dependent on the cooperation between different departments (especially with top management) and external stakeholders. Any potential bottlenecks, stage-gates, or increased slack times heavily influence the added value of the IPR and can, if not managed appropriately, severely diminish the added value.
3. Mixed Front-office/Back-office activities: some activities are so-called Mixed activities, meaning they require both certain legal-administrative tasks to be accomplished and business considerations to be employed. They themselves do not add value to the IPR. The content of these activities, however, goes beyond the scope of purely administrative and legal.

Let us now see how Back-office and Front-office are interconnected. We will do it by taking a look at the generalized flowchart of interconnected Back-office–Front-office activities, where we take especially a patent-based process as the basis. Harrison and Sullivan (2012) wrote that in order to master the handling of intellectual property to a higher degree (what they call a value hierarchy), not only discipline, organization, and leadership are needed but also a roadmap, to see the practices as well as to be able to avoid some mistakes and find gaps in own processes. For that purpose they, for example, present their map of how companies systematically manage and extract value from their intellectual assets. A *caveat* is needed at this point due to the fact that no company uses an IPR process identical to the one shown below—the flow being built on the combination of different theoretical and practical inputs. We suggest the interpretative framework describing the IPR process more in detail (also based on some practices of IPR experts we interviewed): the flowchart, its sub-processes and activities, as well as the role description, depend on the individual settings inside organizations. This means, for example, some activities will be bunched together or that sometimes various functions will be performed by the same person. What is important is that the company has these roles identified, no matter if they are carried out by employee(s) or external consultant(s).

The flowchart above (Fig. 6.6) depicts a mid-level overview of a typical IPRM process as the overall flowchart showing more detailed activities is very complex (and is shown broken down into various sub-processes). The flowchart aims to present the key links between specific activities and their flow (parallel or sequential). The IPRM process consists of six sub-processes, involving various departments, employees, and external consultants.

The first sub-process is IP creation sub-process where the IPRM process begins and where early harvesting of technologies is of utmost importance. Many similarities can be drawn between this and flows depicting development processes or also development stage-gate model. Note the original stage-gate model by Cooper (1998) did not define this stage (often dubbed as discovery). In the IP pre-evaluation sub-process, a number of questions are answered in terms of coreness, crowdedness (in terms of third party patent rights to similar technologies or to components of the technology), alignment with product strategy (considering IP market options), and IPR evaluation leading to decisions on both market relevance and whether or not to apply for a patent or keep the technology as a trade secret. The IPR registration sub-process is the most analysed one, where numerous academics, as well as IPR offices, tend to present simplified versions (at the very least)—especially of the activities that are directly connected to IP offices. The next sub-process is the commercialization, depicting various activities connected to either using IPR as negative rights and as insurance for freedom to operate or utilizing them on the IPR markets (in broad terms because they can be used as a basis for IPR-based cooperation, etc.). The last two sub-processes are enforcement and post-evaluation. The first makes sure that the theoretical comparative edge the IPR brings is not in jeopardy in practice. The second one makes sure that the IPR portfolio remains as active as possible or, in other words, that pruning of the portfolio takes place (see also the section on strategic IPRM).

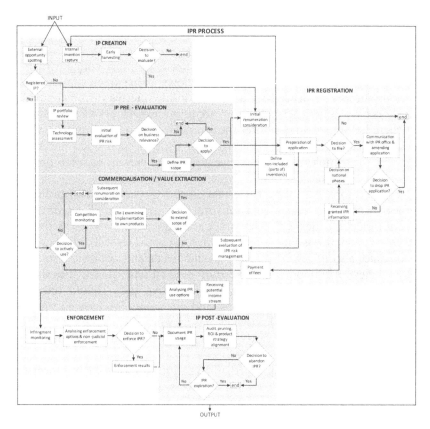

Fig. 6.6   IPR process flowchart (mid-level)

I think one big issue/…/is to detect infringements of IP rights outside in the market. This part is not systematically covered yet. I would like to have more marketing people and development people that are able to indicate where there might be a possible patent infringement. In that way we could make sure we use our patents to realize the value in the patent. That does not always have to be a lawsuit; it can be a license contract, it can be an exchange contract, etc.

> *Senior Vice-President, Chief IP Counsel,*
> *German conglomerate manufacturing and electronics company*

When (re-)evaluating, we have to think about the protection for the entire life cycle, i.e. competitive products that may become cheaper and those cheaper versions being chosen over our products by the consumers.

Head of Legal Operations and IP Management,
European multinational pharmaceutical company

We can see here in Fig. 6.7 that the flow is far more complex than is usually seen when looking at simplified flows, either those presented by various authors or (if we have a chance) inside internal documentations. Authors have nonetheless taken into account various flows that were given to them before, during, or after the interviews by some of the interviewees. The feedback loops and the fact that the process is not a linear one increase the complexity and also have urged us to present each sub-process separately later on.

Furthermore, here we can see that all sub-processes consist of Front-office, Back-office, and Mixed activities. About 33% of all activities are Front-office activities, 32% Back-office activities, and 35% Mixed activities. As mentioned, this is a model flow; hence, the activities will differ between companies also in regard to their specific needs and available resources. Nonetheless, it is important to keep in mind all types of activities should be taken into account and legal-administrative tasks should often be enriched by business considerations (and *vice versa*). We have a variety of decision-making (gateway) activities as well, when the decision is to either push the IPR forward or not—this should not be limited to just a few instances along the path.

We continue by looking more in depth into individual sub-processes. As figures below will show, each sub-process consists of all three types of activities. In addition, the tabular format also includes information regarding the key (accountable) resources for each activity. Such analysis will enable us to build the IPR process model Activity Table that will also structure all resources according to the department they belong to. Every activity in the flowcharts is presented in one of two shapes: either as a rectangle demonstrating those activities that, once executed, automatically proceed to the next activities or as a diamond presenting gateways or activities, where decisions need to be made in order to proceed.

Below (Fig. 6.8) we can see firstly two sources often mentioned by top IPR executives: internal invention capture and subsequent spotting and external opportunity spotting (in line with the notions of open innovations, which are often mentioned by the IPR executives). At the same time, it can serve us as a reminder of the lacking ability of linear models to capture nonlinear invention-related (and IPR-related) processes and activities. Let's take a closer look. The invention reports enable the invention

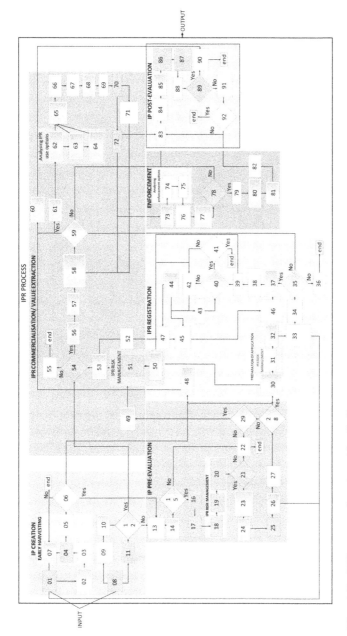

Fig. 6.7 IPR process flowchart (detailed)

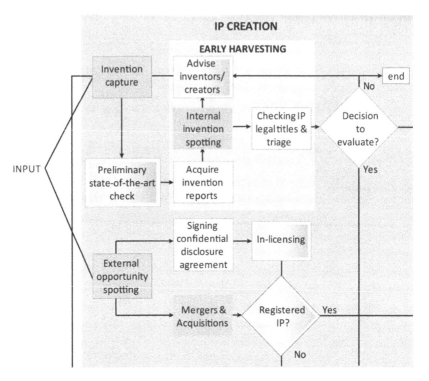

Fig. 6.8 IPR sub-process IP creation flowchart

spotting contained inside the invention report. On the other hand, it can also trigger spotting inventions that have not (yet) made it inside a specific invention report, as invention reports can point out a certain field of work or a certain research group that is not yet a subject of an invention report. This way additional potentially useful inventions might be detected by the IP coordinator or technology manager. IPR process is in its essence an agile process—we may find many feedback loops, which need to be considered also when designing IPR practices. We can also see that there are two activities requiring decisions (or in other words two stage- or toll-gates) inside this IPR sub-process, with the main one deciding on whether or not to continue into the IPR pre-evaluation sub-process.

Furthermore, you can see the activities are divided into three types: Back, Front, and Mixed. The Back-office activities are coloured white, the Front-office processes blue, and Mixed processes are a mix of blue and white. It is clear from this figure that they are intertwined. More specifics can be seen from Table 6.1. A property table is usually developed at the same time as a flowchart, Activity Table, or other graphical presentation. As described in detail in Chap. 3, the property table (or second part of Activity Table) is used to further describe the IPR process behaviour; specifically, Table 6.1 describes IPRM sub-process IP creation behaviour through the identification of key characteristics such as short activity description, input, output, activity type, and its definition. The names of activities (see columns in the table) in the first sub-process are followed by a short preliminary description. This is followed by general input (activity triggers) and outputs (creations) of individual activities. Also notable is the fact that interim outputs are used for activities later on. If we look at the activity decision to evaluate, then this activity is also using outputs from the inventor capture activity, acquisition of invention reports activity, and checking legal titles activity. Interim results are also useful for other processes in the company. Their diffusion to other sub-processes will be especially seen after or during so-called enabling activities, such as the mentioned decision to evaluate. Gateway activities usually do not have a value on their own, but have a critical influence on the continuation of the process as well as gates to transfer the interim results of the IPR processes to other (business) processes in the company.

We focus now on the second sub-process: the pre-evaluation (Fig. 6.9). The sub-process is oriented towards evaluating the technology in terms of both the suitability of using formal (or informal) mechanisms of protection (taking into consideration also the already existing IP portfolio) and its connected business relevance. Let us look a bit more in depth into the checking detectability activity as a Mixed activity. Detectability is the key factor in both deciding on which protection mechanism (formal or informal) to use and also an important element of valuing and rating inventions. The companies might use a simple qualitative-based scale while implementing the expertise knowledge in the field at hand (consult also Box 6.1).

An important group of activities are those connected with IPR risk management. This is, as described in previous chapters, an important part of IPR management, which has two levels: the strategic level and the operational level. In the flowchart below, the operational level can be seen, and in Chap. 7 more details are given on each of these activities. Furthermore, we can see four gateway activities; the first one is a deliberation on whether or not it is worth engaging in a more in-depth analysis of a certain IPR—as

Table 6.1 Property table of IPRM sub-process IP creation

Sub-process	No.	Activity	Short description	Input	Output	Activity type	Activity type definition
IP creation	01.	Invention capture	Transformation of tacit to explicit (from "mind to paper") knowledge done by R&D associate (or in case of trademark marketing employee, or in case of design employee) overseen by IP coordinator		Report on invention, invention timestamp	FO	Business-oriented activity—involved people
	02.	Preliminary state-of-the-art check	The activity is done by the R&D associate (technological invention) as the first input into the innovativeness of the idea looking both at IPR databases and the most noticeable comparables in the market	Report on invention	State-of-the-art report	MIX	Legal-administrative activity, connected also with business considerations
	03.	Acquire invention reports	IP coordinator collects and catalogues filed invention reports	Report on invention with state-of-the-art	List of invention reports	BO	Administrative activity
	04.	Internal invention spotting	Inside this activity (which may also be a feedback-loop activity), the IP coordinator assists the technology manager to recognize potentially valuable inventions		List of harvested inventions, list of suggested new invention reports	FO	
	05.	Checking IP legal titles & triage	Preliminary check of competitive legal titles by the IP coordinator and the patent attorney enabling the necessary input into the next stage-gate activity	Report on invention with state-of-the-art	Legal title report	BO	Legal activity

(continued)

Table 6.1 (continued)

Sub-process	No.	Activity	Short description	Input	Output	Activity type	Activity type definition
	06.	Decision to evaluate	This is a stage-gate activity where IP coordinator decides either to push the invention towards IP portfolio review or to conclude/archive the invention report	Report on invention with state-of-the-art and legal title, list of invention reports		MIX	Enabling activity (gateway), narrow decision-making, no value on its own but has critical influence on the continuation of the process
	07.	Advise inventors/creators	Inside this feedback-loop activity, R&D associate (or marketing employee or design employee) receives advice during the creation process by the IP coordinator and/or patent attorney and/or technology manager. This enables product strategy and IP strategy aligned from this early stage on		Legal & technology advice	MIX	Task's content is in the sphere of legal and technology advice; however, the value lies in product improvement and broader FTO
	08.	External opportunity spotting	Companies not suffering under the Not Invented Here syndrome engage variety of employees to identify usable inventions outside the company	List of external IPR opportunities	List of external IPR opportunities	FO	Business oriented—involved people
	09.	Signing confidential disclosure agreement	The licensing process is accompanied by signing the NDA prepared by the legal expert	In-licensing NDA		BO	Legal activity

(continued)

Table 6.1 (continued)

Sub-process	No.	Activity	Short description	Input	Output	Activity type	Activity type definition
	10.	In-licensing	Technology scout classifies the spotted in-licensing opportunities with the legal input and support from the patent attorney; the activity ends with the signing of the in-licensing agreement by the head R&D dept.	List of external IPR opportunities, in-licensing NDA	Signed in-licence	MIX	Legal-administrative activity with business considerations
	11.	Mergers & acquisitions	Technology scout together with business development expert spots potential mergers & acquisitions that could add value to the internal IPR portfolio. The process is supported by the legal experts and the CEO and CSO		Acquired company with IP	FO	Business oriented—involved people
	12.	Registered IP?	This is an enabling activity (gateway), performed by the head of IP together with the patent attorney, as it consists of assessing the (legal and business) value of the acquired IP rights	Acquired company with IP		MIX	Enabling activity (gateway), narrow decision-making, no value on its own but has critical influence on the continuation of the process

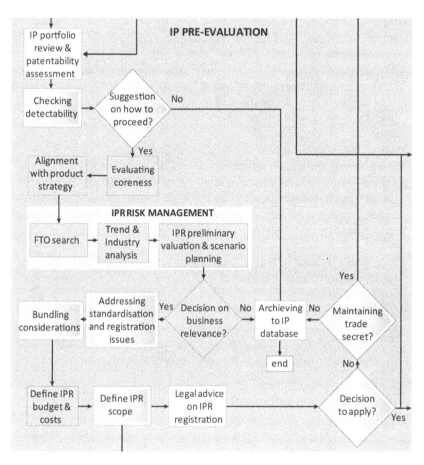

Fig. 6.9 IPR sub-process IP pre-evaluation flowchart

it involves both legal and administrative tasks as well as business considerations, it is a Mixed activity. The second is a Front-office activity as it is a
deliberation on the business relevance. Usually, determining the relevant
potential value of the IPR in general involves two steps. The first part is to
match it with the company's business strategy and desired goals. The second part is to quantify the value it expects the IPR (either through the
product or process implementation/exploitation or some other modus of
IPR exploitation) will provide. The answers to the related questions are
found inside the activities of the evaluating coreness and alignment with

Box 6.1 Checking detectability at a German multinational industrial conglomerate

The respondents have also provided authors with some additional internal materials or have been kind enough to direct us to freely available web sources produced by them. Although not directly citing them, we use them in certain parts inside this monograph to either supplement the information gained inside the interviews or we use them to show certain specific points. What is often seen from the internal material—which is also used inside internal training efforts (see more on training in the continuation of this monograph)—is that the companies strive to present the process in a simplified manner for easier understanding.

This example is taken from our case of the company that is on the list of MIT's most innovative companies. They are also one of the examples that have in recent years established a separate company to handle their IPR (as mentioned before, we have several companies that have decided to do so, like Panasonic). Their detectability scale is simple and contains three values: hard, medium, and easy.

1. *Hard*: Information can only be gathered with great difficulty; additional know-how or background information need to be collected directly from the competitor.
2. *Medium*: Information is available only constrictively and involves major costs and/or efforts (e.g. through more or less complex reverse engineering).
3. *Easy*: Information is publicly available without involving major costs and/or effort by, for example, engaging in web searches, visiting fairs open to public, reading publications or articles.

The scale helps decide on the best route to protect the invention at hand.

the product strategy (as well partially in those connected with risk assessment). The next two are again Mixed activities: the first acting as a gateway to the sub-process of IPR registration and the second showing the involvement of IPR staff when the decision is made to use trade secrets and not IPRs, leading to the commercialization sub-process directly. As we said before, IPR management's primary focus is the IPRs, and trade secrets are taken into consideration mostly when connected with issues of IPRs or when a deliberate decision is made to use non-formal protection mechanisms as substitutes.

We can see (Table 6.2) this sub-process involves both Back-office (administrative and legal) and Front-office (business consideration) activities. Furthermore, we can see from the description of activities there are a variety of people involved from all parts of the company. As we will see in the continuation as well as more in depth in Chap. 7, this involvement of different individuals is quite desirable. This is especially the case when different departments are not aware of the importance of the IPRs or are less interested in them.

We now turn our focus to the next sub-process of IPR registration (Fig. 6.10). The group of activities related to preparing the application takes place immediately after the mixed activity determines the relevant geographic scope. The intermediate output is also later used for determining the national phases (activity: preparation for national phases) as well for the clearance and invalidity search. Also note another feedback loop; after drafting claims, some non-included aspects of the inventions (or at that moment sometimes called background information) can remain. These can either not be dealt with, or they may be systematically thought about and re-entered into the earlier sub-processes. This allows for more efficiency of the process and the information role of IPR management as the IPR process reliance on explicit knowledge, hence knowledge in a form that can be easily transferred and reused at a later time (the formalized processes feature of IPRM). Many of the activities that follow presume the interaction with the patent (IPR) office, either national or not. Respondents have pointed out the importance of acknowledging and reacting to office's feedback as well as utilizing their services in order to improve the IPR registration.

> *SMEs need to understand the nature of the patent filings. You file your patent application in the first country and have 12 months to file elsewhere. Inside our company I strongly encourage that we get searches done by a patent office during that year. Firstly, we have an opportunity to find competing patent applications if prior art is discovered. Secondly, if we find "killer" prior art then we can abandon the application quickly before significant costs are incurred. There are several patent offices, e.g. the British patent office, where you can get a search and examination for around 200 pounds. That is a very low cost. It is an incredibly good investment and most firms can afford it. This is also one opportunity for law firms to do their clients a favour by encouraging them to proceed with this.*

Table 6.2 Property table of IPRM sub-process IP pre-evaluation

Sub-process	No.	Activity	Short description	Input	Output	Activity type	Activity type definition
IP pre-evaluation	13.	IP portfolio review & patentability assessment	The IP coordinator and portfolio innovation manager (or alternatively the head of IP department) position the invention investigated inside the IP portfolio in regard to how the invention enriches the current IP portfolio and IP coordinator assesses the patentability	Report on invention with state-of-the-art and legal title, list of invention reports	IP portfolio review report	BO	Legal, administrative task
	14.	Checking detectability	Involved employees assess the ability of other organizations to uncover the invention at hand and based on that suggest either a formal or informal mechanism of protection	Report on invention with state-of-the-art and legal title	Report on detectability with suggestion on best formal or informal protection mechanism	MIX	Legal, ensuring efficient choice of invention protection, involved people
	15.	Suggestion on how to proceed?	Following the results of the previous pre-evaluation IP activities, the IP coordinator decides either to push the invention forward and what mechanism of protection should be used (hence if formal mechanism should be used) or archive it to the IP database	IP portfolio review, notice of IPR requirements, report on detectability		MIX	Enabling activity (gateway), narrow decision-making, no value on its own but has critical influence on the continuation of the process

(continued)

Table 6.2 (continued)

Sub-process	No.	Activity	Short description	Input	Output	Activity type	Activity type definition
	16.	Evaluating coreness	The technology manager assisted by the IP coordinator assesses the importance of invention in terms of the current R&D goals and the company's current operation.	Report on invention with state-of-the-art and legal title, IP portfolio review	Report on coreness	FO	Identifying importance of invention
	17.	Alignment with product strategy	Employees inside the R&D and marketing department and the IP coordinator assess whether or not the invention is aligned with the product strategy and the company's current and future operations	Report on invention with state-of-the-art and legal title, report on coreness	Opinion on product alignment	FO	Making sure that everything is aligned, connected
	18.	FTO search	Could also be called competitors & FTO search, with patent engineer working with others preparing the FTO opinion	Report on invention with state-of-the-art and legal title, report on coreness	FTO opinion, market research, investment allowance	FO	Business oriented—involved people
	19.	Trend and industry analysis	IP coordinator together with marketing employee prepares the trend and industry analysis	FTO opinion, market research, investment allowance	Trend & industry report	FO	Business oriented—involved people
	20.	IPR preliminary valuation & scenario planning	The employees preliminary valuate the IPR and prepare scenarios. The output is used also in the next enabling activities	Report on invention with state-of-the-art and legal title	Preliminary valuation document & scenario	FO	Business oriented—involved people

(continued)

Table 6.2 (continued)

Sub-process	No.	Activity	Short description	Input	Output	Activity type	Activity type definition
	21.	Decision on business relevance?	This critical enabling activity is done seeking wide approval	FTO report, market research, investment allowance, trend & industry report, pitch on business relevance		FO	Enabling activity (gateway), decision-making with multiple entities involved, has critical influence on the continuation of the process
	22.	Archiving to IP database	If the invention is not pushed further, the IP coordinator archives the IP	Report on invention with state-of-the-art and legal title	IP database entry	BO	Administrative task
	23.	Addressing standardization and registration issues	The legal expert addresses the administrative side, while the R&D associate and sales employee are responsible for the business consideration regarding possible standardization issues that may influence the IPR	Market research, report on invention with state-of-the-art and legal title, trend & industry report	Report on standardization	MIX	Administrative task connected also with business considerations
	24.	Bundling considerations	All employees check possible bundling of the IP, with other inventions as well as other IPR (including potentially needed further in-licensing)	IP portfolio review report, report on invention with state-of-the-art and legal title	Opinion on bundling opportunities	MIX	Product oriented (protection of all aspects of invention) based on legal expertise
	25.	Define IPR budget & costs	IPR budget & costs are defined by all involved employees, the activity being coordinated by the IP coordinator	Preliminary valuation, opinion on bundling opportunities	Business case, IPR budget estimations	FO	Business oriented—involved people

(continued)

Table 6.2 (continued)

Sub-process	No.	Activity	Short description	Input	Output	Activity type	Activity type definition
	26.	Define IPR scope	All involved in the creation of the invention, the coordination, the research (either the patent engineer inside the IP(R) department or the R&D associate inside the R&D department), as well as those providing IPR legal expertise need to work together to define the optimal scope of the intellectual property right	Report on invention with state-of-the-art and legal title, opinion on bundling opportunities, trend & industry report	IPR scope	MIX	Product oriented (protection of all aspects of invention) based on legal expertise
	27.	Legal advice on IPR registration	Based on previous activities, the patent attorney provides his legal opinion on viability of the IPR registration	Report on invention with state-of-the-art, legal title and IPR scope, opinion on bundling opportunities	Advice on registration	BO	Legal task
	28.	Decision to apply?	Both involved employees decide whether or not to proceed with the IPR registration	Business case, advice on registration, IPR budget estimation		MIX	Enabling activity (gateway), decision-making with multiple entities involved, has critical influence on the continuation of the process
	29.	Maintain trade secret?	IP coordinator, patent attorney, and technology manager deliberate on maintaining the technology as a trade secret	Business case, advice on registration		MIX	Enabling activity (gateway), decision-making with multiple entities involved, has critical influence on the continuation of the process

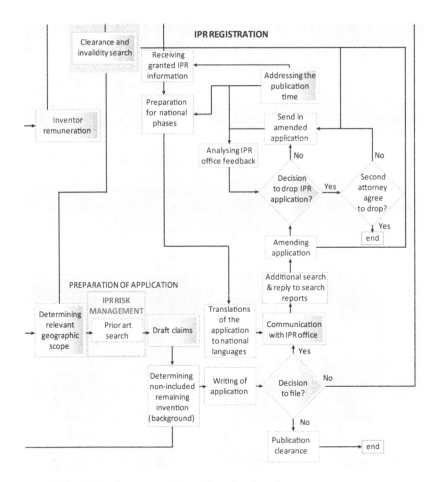

Fig. 6.10 IPR sub-process IPR registration flowchart

In this way innovations and IPR processes are taking advantage of the numerous mechanisms available these days to get early patent office input. Some companies find out, inside those first 12 months, that they are never going to get a useful patent protection and realize it is best not to proceed. That is useful as it prevents future higher costs.

This is also something I encourage strongly inside our company. Utilizing those options can be extremely good value for money.

Head of Legal Operations and IP Management,
European multinational pharmaceutical company

Note also the loop that connects first application with decisions on subsequent application processes—we do not delve extensively into this as the topics are widely covered both in literature and in other sources (online, etc.). Still, please consult the next few lines (focusing on the patent application) to gain an insight into the IPR process itself as some activities subsume some of the previous considerations. Most commonly the patent will be first applied for in the applicant's home country. The applicant then has an additional 12 months after the date of the first application (so-called priority date) to apply for patents in additional countries. What are those additional countries? There are two situations here: the applicant might have a pretty good idea where they want to file—according to his market needs. Alternatively, the applicant might need time to think—in that case the Patent Cooperation Treaty (PCT) application is often a useful option. Again, it needs to be done in the 12 months of the priority data; nonetheless a broad list of countries can be identified in this filing—allowing the applicant to gain more time to identify their market needs or determine the suitable geographical dimension of exploitation options for the patent. Also, as part of the PCT application, it can determine the European Patent Office (EPO)—where again countries can be determined (but note, this is always an elimination process). Hence, the loop in Fig. 6.10 can repeat itself several times (with or without all the steps determined).

Another very important part of the IPR registration process is connected with the communication with the IPR office. After the initial filing, several office actions will follow—it is important to be ready for them also in terms of available resources to dedicate to this, as it will determine the scope (and strength) of your patent. Among the most important is the so-called search report—specifying existing prior art. This report will elicit an additional response, sometimes including the amendment of the application. When a patent examiner issues an office action that refuses to allow all claims (using either the wording rejection or objection), they have not rejected the invention as such. However, it is also a point, where sufficient feedback is gathered in relation to the patentability of the invention—hence another decision point is reached in which it is deliberated whether or not to continue with the patenting process. Within 18 months, a patent is made public. The applicant has to make a decision to continue the application process or not and request a so-called ("substantive") examination—as well as designate countries—hence the patent will then reach the so-called national phases. All in all, the understanding of the process will ensure that the optimal scope, cost, and time scheme can be achieved.

We would expect the majority of the activities to be Back-office activities, due to the fact this is a highly formalized sub-process (see Table 6.3).

Table 6.3 Property table of IPRM sub-process IP registration

Sub-process	No.	Activity	Short description	Input	Output	Activity type	Activity type definition
IP registration	30.	Determining geographic scope	The portfolio manager and patent attorney suggest the geographic scope for the IPR taking into consideration the input by the sales	Business case	Opinion on geographical scope	MIX	Legal task, enriched with business considerations on efficient IPR protection
	31.	Prior art search	Inside the IPR registration work process, extensive prior art search is conducted	Report on invention with state-of-the-art, legal title and IPR scope, opinion on geographical scope	Prior art report	BO	Legal task
	32.	Draft claims	The patent attorney drafts claims based on R&D associate's or patent engineer's input; the final confirmation given by the head of IP department or someone who was given the authority to do so	Report on invention with prior art, legal title and IPR scope	Written claims	MIX	Legal, ensuring sufficient scope of invention protection, involved people
	33.	Determining non-included remaining invention (background)	Inside this activity the remaining know-how or background information is defined and a decision is made on how to utilize and protect it. This is again a feedback-loop activity as the remains can be subject to additional IPR scope or enriching the archive of available inventions	Written claims	Proposal on handling the remaining parts of invention (not covered by the written claims)	BO	Legal-administrative task

(continued)

Table 6.3 (continued)

Sub-process	No.	Activity	Short description	Input	Output	Activity type	Activity type definition
	34.	Writing of application	The patent attorney finalizes the IPR application based on R&D associate's input	Prior art report, written claims, notice of geographical scope	IPR application	BO	Legal task
	35.	Decision to file	Based on the input compiled by the IP coordinator, IP portfolio information provided by the portfolio innovation manager, and the patent attorney's IPR expertise, the decision whether to file or not is made	Business case, IPR application		MIX	Legal, administrative task connected with business consideration; enabling activity (gateway)
	36.	Publication clearance	Before either R&D associate, marketing, or sales employee in any way publicize either the invention or the IPR, the IP coordinator needs to issue the publication clearance	Business case, IPR application	Publication notification	BO	Administrative task
	37.	Communication with IPR office	During the IP application process, various issues pointed out by the IP office need to be cleared (involving technical, legal, or financial issues)	IPR office examiners' written and oral feedback (including possible interview with the patent examiner)	Submitting responses to IP office actions: corrected objections, amendments in claims, overcoming (obviousness or novelty) rejections	MIX	Legal-administrative task, connected with people

(continued)

Table 6.3 (continued)

Sub-process	No.	Activity	Short description	Input	Output	Activity type	Activity type definition
	38.	Additional search & reply to search reports	Based on IP office feedback, additional search and examination are performed by the employees	IPR office feedback and own responses	Search & examination report	BO	Legal task, administrative task
	39.	Amending application	Based on IP office feedback, the patent attorney amends the application (sometimes aided by the patent engineer)	IPR office feedback, search & examination report	Amended application	BO	Legal task
	40.	Decision to drop IPR application	Based on IP office feedback and the input by the technology manager, patent attorney can decide to drop the IPR application	IPR office feedback, amended application		MIX	Legal, administrative task connected with business consideration; enabling activity. (gateway)
	41.	Second attorney agree to drop?	A second attorney's revision is also an enabling activity as it may conclude/end the process of IPR application	IPR office feedback, amended application, decision to drop IPR application		BO	Legal task; enabling activity (gateway)
	42.	Send in amended application	Patent attorney sends the amended IPR application to the IP office	Amended application	Consequent amended application, IPR document	BO	Legal task
	43.	Analysing IPR office feedback	The IP office feedback is analysed by the IP coordinator, patent attorney, and either the R&D associate or the patent engineer	IPR office feedback	Opinion IP office feedback	BO	Legal task

(continued)

Table 6.3 (continued)

Sub-process	No.	Activity	Short description	Input	Output	Activity type	Activity type definition
	44.	Addressing the publication time	This legal task is performed by the patent attorney and based on business input by the rest of the involved employees	Business case	Notice on early publication	MIX	Legal task, enriched with business considerations on efficient IPR protection
	45.	Preparation for national phases	Preparations in regard to entrance to national phases by the involved employees	IPR document	National phase preliminary documentation	BO	Legal task, administrative task
	46.	Translations of the application to national languages	The patent attorney with the help of the R&D associate coordinates the translation of the application to national languages	IPR document	Translation	BO	Administrative task
	47.	Receiving granted IPR information	The IPR grant is received and reviewed by the IP coordinator, patent attorney, and R&D associate	IPR office award notice	IPR title, grant timestamp	BO	Administrative task
	48.	Inventor remuneration	Head and IPP coordinator provide input on the innovators' efforts; legal expert and finance employee are involved with the execution of the employee remuneration, based on the COO decision	Business case, IPR office award notice, invention report	Contract on remuneration	MIX	Legal, administrative task connected with business consideration

Nonetheless, added value of IPRM involves several business-oriented considerations, which is mirrored in several Mixed activities. For example, the gateway activity decision to drop an application is in its essence a legal-administrative task, which however cannot be done without serious business considerations evaluating if and when additional benefits are to be or not to be expected from the IPR under scrutiny. Furthermore, as this is one of the key enabling activities that leads either to the end of the IPRM process or to the continuation of the process, respondents also point out some additional activities that could be incorporated, if the resources allow the companies to do so, such as seeking the opinion of a second patent attorney.

The sub-process of IP commercialization (Fig. 6.11)—the term being interchangeable with the term exploitation—is where we can see that IPRM can go beyond the product development or production process, or what is more so the focus of IPM. Indeed, most companies will try to protect the IP and IPRs that are connected to products they deliver to the goods market. Nonetheless, further consideration needs to be taken—making the decision to extend the scope of IPR use one of the key decision points. Of course, there are examples when using the IPRs on the market for ideas as the main modus of extracting value from IPRs from the beginning, but it is limited to specific cases: either to the phase in which a certain company has found itself or the business model it is pursuing.

> *In a dying company, which does not sell their products anymore, that [presence on IPR market] might also be the focus. The only chance to make a return on the investment from past R&D is to license or sell their patents. So there are moments when things are turned around.*
>
> *Chief IP Counsel,*
> *German international automotive supplier*

Hence, the commercialization or exploitation (some call it also value capture) process is a natural follow-on step on the road to extracting value from IPR. This is also the step that gets us closer to the end outputs (and not just interim results/outputs). As we have already discussed, there are various ways this value can be extracted; Harrison and Sullivan (2012) point out the following "list"—we add here the ones that pertain to our commercialization phase: (1) to productize the IPR, utilizing IPR to protect new product features (or introduce a process innovation, which Harrison and Sullivan (2012) do not point out); (2) to monetize the patent, obtaining revenue directly from the use of IPR in a licence or other

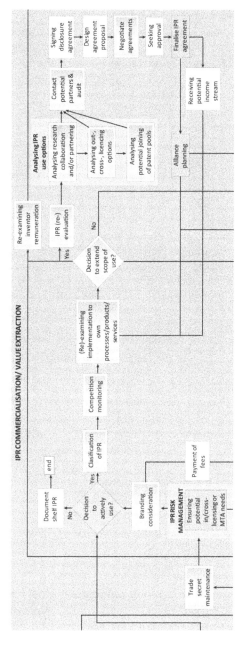

Fig. 6.11 IPR sub-process IP commercialization flowchart

value-generating use; and (c) to use it for positioning purposes, using the IPR for competitive blocking, to create barriers to competitive entry and to enhance company reputation. Here both the signalling value and the potential use for IPR-based cooperation come to the forefront (see also Chaps. 2 and 3 for a more theoretical introduction to this). Figure 6.11 shows several options of extracting value from an IPR and the activities (and activity flow itself) will follow the desired goals.

As we can see from Table 6.4, the emphasis inside the IP commercialization sub-process is on Front-office activities and Mixed activities. Business considerations inside this sub-process are especially strong on all levels, including how and to what dedicate more resources inside this sub-process.

> *We have an internal ranking system for our cases. An A, B, C rating; which could be regarded as another IP asset management tool. We classify them as A: strategic, B: could potentially cover one of our products and C: defensive. From an IP asset management perspective, your attorney should be spending more of their time on the A cases and less time on the C cases. And we try to do that, nonetheless there are so many ways to evaluate and rate. For example, you could be looking at what is linked to a product now on the market, what is already licensed or is licensable.*
>
> Head of Legal Operations and IP Management,
> European multinational pharmaceutical company

The decision to actively use a granted patent is not an entirely autonomous decision as it is highly dependent on the underlying R&D and commercialization process. Nonetheless, inside the IPR process, it is a necessary milestone, as sometimes the patent is granted, whereas there was a hitch in the commercialization process and the patent may be turned into a shelf patent. On the other hand, the company may seek other options to exploit such IPR. The group of activities titled Analysing IPR use options is in this sense especially focal as it allows discovering further exploitation options. Certainly, further exploitation options may be sought also when the IPR is also embedded in their own product or processes; however, it will be done with a raised degree of caution. For some of the commercialization options, the final activity, which embodies the goal, is the receiving of the income. Interestingly, although much thought goes to negotiating the potential income stream generating agreements, there is less thought given to their monitoring. If there is, there are two types of resources that can be utilized: internal with internal royalty audit professional and

Table 6.4 Property table of IPRM sub-process IP commercialization

Sub-process	No.	Activity	Short description	Input	Output	Activity type	Activity type definition
IPR commercialization/ value extraction	49.	Trade secret maintenance	IP coordinator, technology manager, and legal expert form the trade secret plan	Business case	Trade secret plan	MIX	Legal task, enriched with business considerations on efficient IPR protection
	50.	Clearance and invalidity search	The IP coordinator either organizes the clearance and invalidity search with in-house patent attorney and patent engineer or he or the head of the IP department is the contact point for outside organizations conducting this search	Notice on geographical scope, prior art report, IPR application, FTO opinion, market research	Clearance and invalidity report	MIX	Legal, administrative task connected with business consideration; in essence is also an enabling activity (gateway) as it feeds into and effects R&D and commercialization process as well as IPR application
	51.	Ensuring potential in-/ cross-licensing or MTA needs	Potential need for complementary IPR is assessed	IPR document, IP portfolio landscape	In-, cross- licensing needs opinion	FO	Product oriented
	52.	Payment of fees	The finance employee pays the fees	IPR office notice	Bank statement	BO	Administrative task
	53.	Branding/design consideration	Enhancing the utility of the IPR done by the marketing employee, sales employee, and IP coordinator	Business case, IPR office award notice	Branding report	FO	Administrative task connected also with business considerations
	54.	Decision to actively use	The decision if the IPR will be actively pursued as well as how it could be utilized is made with a wide consensus	IPR classification report, in-/ cross-licensing opinion		FO	Business oriented— involved people

(continued)

Table 6.4 (continued)

Sub-process	No.	Activity	Short description	Input	Output	Activity type	Activity type definition
	55.	Document shelf IPR	If the IPR is not actively used, the IP coordinator archives the related documentation	IPR office award notice	IPR database entry	BO	Administrative task
	56.	Classification of IPR	The granted IPR is classified in 1 to 3 A, B, C or similar categories based on business prospects of the IPR	IPR office award notice	IPR classification entry	MIX	Product oriented, involved people, includes legal, administrative aspects
	57.	Competition monitoring	During the commercialization work process, a variety of employees are engaged in monitoring other companies' activities related to the registered IP	IPR office award notice with classification	Report on competitors	MIX	Administrative task connected also with business considerations, output for internal stakeholders
	58.	(Re-)examining implementation to own processes/products/services	Based on the financial and tax estimation prepared by the finance department and the input of the technology manager, the issue of further internal exploitation of the IPR is examined	Report on competitors, IPR office award notice with classification	Report on further internal use, financial & tax estimation	MIX	Administrative task connected also with business considerations with business outputs
	59.	Decision to extend scope of use	The decision is made to pursue other possible value generation uses of the IPR	Report on further internal use, financial & tax estimation		MIX	Business considerations influenced also by administrative and legal considerations

(continued)

Table 6.4 (continued)

Sub-process	No.	Activity	Short description	Input	Output	Activity type	Activity type definition
	60.	Re-examining inventor remuneration	Based on two types of input ((1) on the innovator's efforts provided by the head and IP coordinator and (2) on the business effect of the IPR), the COO re-examines the remuneration assisted by the legal expert and finance employee	Contract on remuneration	Amended contract on remuneration	MIX	Legal, administrative task connected with business consideration
	61.	IPR (re-) evaluation	The input for the primary evaluation is gathered widely and is also reliant on some previous outputs—more or less developed metrics can be employed or a comparable approach	Report on further internal use, financial & tax estimation	Valuation document	MIX	Business oriented—involved people
	62.	Analysing further research collaboration and/or partnering	The involved employees examine the external option for IPR-based collaboration and partnering	Report on use with valuation	Analysis on further research collaboration and/or partnering	MIX	Administrative task connected also with business considerations with business outputs
	63.	Analysing out-licensing options	Based on the input of the R&D associate and/or the technology manager, the strategic sales manager and/or the sales employee examine future out-licensing options	Analysis on further research collaboration and/or partnering	Analysis on out-licensing option, tax &financial estimation	MIX	Administrative task connected also with business considerations with business outputs

(continued)

Table 6.4 (continued)

Sub-process	No.	Activity	Short description	Input	Output	Activity type	Activity type definition
	64.	Analysing potential joining of patent pools	The technology manager, the head of R&D, and the strategic sales manager analyse existing patent pools taking into account the potential financial cost/benefit estimations by the financial employee and in line with the business goals and objectives laid out by the COO	Analysis on further research collaboration and/or partnering	Analysis of potential patent pools	MIX	Administrative task connected also with business considerations with business outputs
	65.	Contact potential partners & audit	The employee who has previous contact with the potential partner starts the conversations. Audit is performed	Analysis on further research collaboration and/ or partnering, analysis on out-licensing option, analysis of potential patent pools	Established contacts, letter of intent, audit report	MIX	Administrative task connected also with business considerations
	66.	Signing disclosure agreement	Legal expert drafts the necessary NDA	Audit report, established contact	NDA with partners	BO	Legal task
	67.	Design agreement proposal	The legal expert together with the strategic sales manager and the portfolio innovation manager drafts the initial agreement provisions	NDA with partners	Initial agreement provisions	BO	Legal task

(continued)

Table 6.4 (continued)

Sub-process	No.	Activity	Short description	Input	Output	Activity type	Activity type definition
	68.	Negotiate agreements	This Back-office/Front-office activity has elements of administrative tasks underneath, although business considerations are dominating the activity, also due to COO's involvement	Initial agreement provisions	Agreement content	MIX	Legal task, enriched with business considerations on efficient IPR protection
	69.	Seeking approval	The aim of this Back-office activity is to gain internal approval for the use of IPR on the IPR market	Agreement content	Approved agreement proposal	BO	Administrative task
	70.	Finalize IPR agreement	The final IPR agreement is signed by the COO as prepared in the final version by the legal expert	Approved agreement proposal	Signed IPR transfer agreement	FO	Business oriented, involved people
	71.	Receiving income stream	The finance department records the income stream generated by an IPR	Signed IPR transfer agreement	Financial statement	BO	Administrative task
	72.	Alliance planning	This Front-office activity is performed by the business development expert (or their team) in order to plan and execute cooperative activities based on IPR	Signed IPR transfer agreement, business case	Alliance-integration plan	FO	Business oriented, involved people

external, where these services are acquired from an external service provider. For commercialization activities not connected to "productizing the IPR" (Harrison and Sullivan 2012), alliance management professionals are of utmost importance. This is due to the fact that finding IPR-based cooperation options and signalling are important goals for such instances.

We turn now to the last two sub-processes depicted in Fig. 6.12: enforcement and IP post-evaluation, respectively. The key activity at the beginning of the enforcement sub-process is infringement monitoring. This can be done with internal as well as outside resources (customers, etc.). The key gateway activity is the decision to either enforce the IPR or not, followed by enforcement negotiations. The real economic value may be (re)determined at that point, as the inability to protect the IPR may dramatically decrease its value as an asset. *Vice versa*, patents are always granted with a presumption of validity—and one of the key tasks of the IPR staff is to keep the IPR valid. No patent (or other IPR) is safe from being challenged and declared invalid (or partially invalid), either inside the IPR registration process (hence, still being a part of communication with the IPR office as so-called pre-issuance submission—the first opportunity arises in the examination proceedings, which however, for strategic reasons, is rarely done (Holzer 2006)) or later as a post-grant opposition or appeal. As in practice the challenge does not come out of the blue; it is usually a reaction to external (or internal) stimuli, for example, an infringement action or contractual dispute. Thus also in those cases similar activities take place as noted below, with activities being somewhat differently named (with the emphasis of defending own existing IPR). The last sub-process, the post-evaluation, is a repeating exercise, which will follow until the IPR is no longer valid or until the decision is made that the IPR is obsolete and cannot be further exploited—not even only as a signal or for strategic purposes.

Table 6.5 shows us the activities of both sub-processes, their type, inputs, and outputs. For the enforcement sub-process to begin, the first activity infringement monitoring needs to produce a report—which can take on various forms—but needs to include at least the basic data on which further analysis can be based on. Truly important outputs of the next activities are the opinion on the scope of infringement and the opposition analysis as these will be the main inputs when deciding on whether to pursue the infringement or not. Also the final output of the last activity in this sub-process needs to be mentioned as the result needs to be documented in some form (and not rely purely on organizational or individual

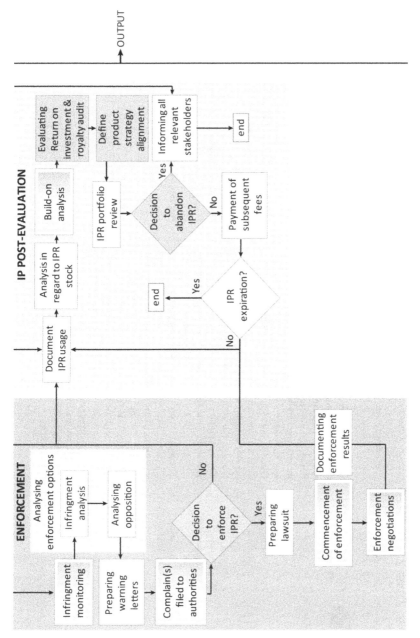

Fig. 6.12 IPR sub-processes enforcement and IP post-evaluation flowchart

Table 6.5 Property table of IPRM sub-processes enforcement and IP post-evaluation

Sub-process	No.	Activity	Short description	Input	Output	Activity type	Activity type definition
Enforcement	73.	Infringement monitoring	Several employees may come across infringements to IPR during performance of their duties; the infringement monitoring can be more or less formalized	IPR use report, alliance-integration plan	Report on infringement	MIX	Administrative task connected also with business considerations
	74.	Infringement analysis	Once an infringement is detected, the employees present an opinion on the scope of the infringement	Report on infringement	Opinion on the scope of infringement	BO	Legal task, administrative task
	75.	Analysing opposition	The infringing entity is analysed by the employees	Report on infringement with scope	Opposition analysis	BO	Legal task, administrative task
	76.	Preparing warning letters	The legal expert together with the patent attorney prepares the warning letter following a detected infringement	Report on infringement with scope, opposition analysis	Warning letter	BO	Legal task, administrative task
	77.	Complain(s) filed to authorities	The innovation portfolio manager and/or head of the IPR department together with the legal department prepare complaints to various authorities to deter the infringement	Report on infringement with scope, opposition analysis	Complains	MIX	Legal-administrative task with business considerations

(continued)

Table 6.5 (continued)

Sub-process	No.	Activity	Short description	Input	Output	Activity type	Activity type definition
	78.	Decision to enforce IPR	The COO or the head of IP decides whether to enforce the IPR based on the input information by the innovation portfolio manager, the head of the R&D, and the legal expert	Scope of infringement, opposition analysis		FO	Business oriented, involved people
	79.	Preparing lawsuit	The legal expert and the patent attorney prepare the lawsuit documentation also taking into account the R&D associate's or technology manager's input	Report on infringement with scope, opposition analysis	Lawsuit	BO	Legal task
	80.	Commencement of enforcement	The legal expert files the lawsuit based on the prior decision of the COO	Report on infringement with scope, opposition analysis, lawsuit	Enforcement documentation	MIX	Legal task, administrative task with business considerations
	81.	Enforcement negotiations	After the filed lawsuit, typically negotiations follow carried out by a smaller team, consisting of the patent attorney, the legal expert, and the COO	Enforcement documentation	Negotiated terms of IPR conflict resolution	MIX	Legal task, business oriented—enriched with business considerations on efficient IPR protection
	82.	Documenting enforcement results	The IP coordinator inserts the new pertaining information in the IP(R) database	Negotiated terms of IPR conflict resolution	Enforcement database entry	BO	Administrative task

(continued)

Table 6.5 (continued)

Sub-process	No.	Activity	Short description	Input	Output	Activity type	Activity type definition
IP post-evaluation	83.	Document IPR usage	The IPR usage is documented by the IP coordinator also following the development manager's and technology manager's input	IPR use report, alliance-integration plan, enforcement database entry	Report on IPR use	BO	Administrative task
	84.	Analysis in regard to IPR stock	The IP coordinator and the portfolio innovation manager examine the IPR as to its relevant position inside the IP(R) portfolio. Follow-up applications are considered to guarantee a continuous IPR protection of certain inventive activities	Report on IPR use, IPR portfolio review	Report on impact on individual IPR in regard to IPR stock	BO	Administrative task
	85.	Build-on analysis	A build-on analysis is performed in the cooperation between the IP coordinator, several employees of the R&D department, and the strategic account manager and design expert	Report on IPR use, IPR portfolio review	Build-on analysis	MIX	Product oriented, involved people, includes legal, administrative aspects

(continued)

Table 6.5 (continued)

Sub-process	No.	Activity	Short description	Input	Output	Activity type	Activity type definition
	86.	Evaluating return on investment & royalty audit	The activity presents one of the most difficult parts of the whole process as the metrics and sometimes also the input parameters are arguable. When IPR is used on IPR market, a royalty audit is performed	Report on IPR use, report on impact on individual IPR in regard to IPR stock	Evaluated ROI	FO	Business oriented, involved people
	87.	Define product strategy alignment	Alignment with the company's product strategy is re-evaluated and the matching re-assessed by the participating employees—this is a very product-oriented activity	Report on IPR use, IPR portfolio review, build-on analysis	Product strategy alignment	FO	Product oriented, involved people
	88.	IPR portfolio review	The IP coordinator and the portfolio innovation manager assess the IPR portfolio in both scenarios: one of dropping the IPR and second of keeping it	Report on IPR use, IPR portfolio review, build-on analysis	IPR portfolio analysis	BO	Administrative task
	89.	Decision to abandon IPR	Based on the inputs from previous activities, a joint meeting is held to deliberate on continuous use or possible abandonment of the IPR	Report on IPR use, build-on analysis, report ROI, product strategy alignment, IPR portfolio analysis		FO	Enabling activity (gateway), decision-making with multiple entities involved, has critical influence on the continuation of the process

(continued)

Table 6.5 (continued)

Sub-process	No.	Activity	Short description	Input	Output	Activity type	Activity type definition
	90.	Informing all relevant stakeholders	IP coordinator informs all relevant stakeholders, especially all departments utilizing the abandonment of the IPR and the inventor	Decision regarding abandonment	Note to stakeholders	BO	Administrative task
	91.	Payment of subsequent fees	The financial expert pays the fees to the appropriate IPR office	IPR office notice	Bank statement	BO	Administrative task
	92.	IPR expiration?	The patent attorney and portfolio innovation manager warn of the expired IPR	IPR office notice	Entry of expiration into IPR database	BO	Administrative task

memory and recall—when we did our analysis of smaller companies, unfortunately this is indeed many times the case).

The last sub-process IP post-evaluation is an interesting mix of Front-office, Back-office, and Mixed activities. In general we can see two types of outputs: does related to the individual IPR and does related to how this IPR helps achieve business goals of the company. One of the important issues before abandoning the IPR is to make sure no part of business uses the IPR in any significant matter. This ensures the IPR would not be abandoned too soon as well as prepares the business to no longer be able to rely on this particular IPR. Please also note that the inputs and outputs are sometimes named in a generalized way, as, for example, the IPR office notice does not imply a "notice" per se but rather the realization of the expiration of the patent.

> *We use this service with a tool from PatentSight GmbH [that you just mentioned] for measuring and assessing the quality of our patent portfolio; and also for the development of our patent portfolio.*
>
> *Senior Vice-President, Chief IP Counsel,*
> *German conglomerate manufacturing and electronics company*

Both flowcharts and tables contain detailed information about each identified activity in the IPR process. By using flowchart and tables, we have not only gained valuable information about activities, where they take place, who is involved in their execution, the inputs and outputs, as well as their type and the reasons behind them, but they will also enable us, together with the human resource table (Fig. 7.1), to structure all information required to build the Activity Table IPR process model that will be presented in Chap. 7.

The aim of Chap. 6 was to *firstly* define the IPRM process characteristics and investigate their contribution to the successful deployment of IPR process in practice. Each of them exposes different aspects of IPRM, either from business strategy, value added, time constraints, or resource perspective. *Secondly*, the strategic IPRM framework emphasis is presented. *Thirdly*, the chapter focused on two key dimensions of IPRM by structuring activities, identified within the IPR process, as either Back-office activities or Front-office activities. It also identified so-called Mixed activities that contain both Back-office and Front-office tasks, for example, checking detectability activity (within the IPR pre-evaluation sub-process) that deals on one hand with legal aspects by ensuring the efficient choice of invention protection and on the other involves resources from marketing, design, and operations departments. *Fourthly*, building on Fig. 5.9, the chapter introduced additional views of IPR process activities. As Fig. 5.9 presents the top-level view of IPR process, figures in this chapter present the middle-level view as well as a detailed view of IPR process. Additionally, each IPR sub-process is not only presented graphically in a form of a flow-chart but also in a tabular form to contribute to the full understanding of every activity. The tables provide a short description of activities, their inputs, outputs, as well as their type. Both the graphical and tabular presentation of IPR process activities will enable us to develop the Activity Table IPR process model that will link the activities with the resources and departments involved in the identified IPR process. The IPR process model will be presented in the following chapter, alongside the answer to question if IPR formalization also brings IPR process optimization.

If the process is diligently organized, then Front-office and Back-office tasks will be intertwined within different IPR sub-processes. An important question arises then: do smaller companies perform all these activities by themselves? The apparent answer is no. Nonetheless, there are important lessons smaller companies can learn from knowledge about the IPR activity flow within their larger competitors because:

1. Using external service providers such as patent attorneys or companies conducting clearance searches on a number of activities (however not all of them) can offer some advantages, yet also some significant disadvantages. Inefficiencies that arise when using external counsel stem from the lack of knowledge about the process, the inability to define the optimal scope of assistance needed as well as optimal timing for acquiring these external services (consider here the issue of timing the clearing activity—if done too early, it may cause issues later—whether due to the need to repeat it or from an unforeseen competitors' reaction). Understanding the IPR process, its activities, their (inter-)connectedness, and processes surrounding them is key to optimizing value extracted from external IPR services—knowledge that we wish to provide.
2. Smaller companies may benchmark and compare their IPR process in order to use it either as a signpost for their redesign of processes or simply to optimize their individual activities.

We need to acknowledge that smaller companies tend to put less emphasis on active management. However, the research shows that:

(1) this is often due to the lack of knowledge, a fact that has been confirmed by research (both WIPO and OECD, etc.); (2) not all smaller companies neglect IPR management—indeed there is proof countering the often stated opinion that smaller (including medium-sized) companies across the field neglect it and rather emphasize heterogeneity across companies (see, e.g. Jell (2012), OECD (2011), Keupp et al. (2009), including our own supplementary research (not part of the present monograph) on small- and medium-sized companies (validating the TAD IPR method on a smaller scale)); (3) even when internal patenting competence is outsourced to external consultants, top management retains central roles regarding patenting decisions, and sole reliance on external IP service providers is not a sufficient substitute for internal expertise (Holgersson 2013); it agrees with some of our ongoing and also past research; (4) some smaller companies put emphasis on being "agile" in terms of IPR, as opposed to having insufficient IPR resources and knowledge. Consequently, they do not even attempt to define the most optimal resources (e.g. Alkaersig et al. 2015) with marketing or sales playing the predominant role.

References

Alkaersig, L., Beukel, K., & Reichstein, T. (2015). *Intellectual property rights management: Rookies, dealers and strategists.* Hampshire: Palgrave.

Cooper, R. G. (1988). *Winning at new products.* London: Kogan Page.

Gassmann, O., & Bader, M. A. (2017). Patentmanagement in der Open Innovation Ära. In O. Gassmann & Bader (Eds.), *Patentmanagement: Innovationen erfolgreich nutzen und schützen.* Berlin and Heidelberg: Springer.

Harrison, S. S., & Sullivan, P. H. (2012). *Edison in the boardroom revisited: How leading companies realize value from their intellectual property: Revisited.* Hoboken, NJ: Wiley.

Holgersson, M. (2013). Patent management in entrepreneurial SMEs: A literature review and an empirical study of innovation appropriation, patent propensity, and motives. *R&D Management, 43*(1), 21–36.

Holzer, W. (2006). Effective mechanisms for challenging the validity of patents. Retrieved from http://www.wipo.int/export/sites/www/meetings/en/2006/scp_of_ge_06/presentations/scp_of_ge_06_holzer.pdf

Jell, F. (2012). *Patent filling strategies and patent management: An empirical study.* Wiesbaden: Gabler Verlag and Springer Fachmedien.

Keupp, M., Lhuillery, S., Garcia-Torres, M. A., & Raffo, J. (2009). *SME-IP: 2nd report economic focus study on SMEs and intellectual property in Switzerland.* Bern: Swiss Federal Institute of Intellectual Property.

OECD. (2011). *Collaborative mechanisms for intellectual property management in the life sciences.* Paris: OECD.

Pavitt, K. (2006). Innovation process. In J. Fagerberg, D. C. Mowery, & R. R. Nelson (Eds.), *The Oxford handbook of innovation.* Oxford: Oxford University Press.

CHAPTER 7

IPR Management in Action: The Road to "Better" IPR Management

Abstract This chapter builds upon the previous chapters and first deals with examining the human resource dimension from the individual and departmental level. The chapter then continues with the practical side of IPRM tools.

Using the TAD IPR model to describe IPRM practices in depth, we also consider what to worry about when (re)designing IPR processes. Hence, the chapter delivers the IPR Activity Table—bringing the activities and the connected administrative, legal, and business considerations. Using the model, we use the tabular method to present the links between the identified activities and resources. The analysis also shows the possible gaps and more appropriate people to carry out the activities.

Keywords Human resources in IPR management • Activity Table • TAD methodology • IPR tools • IPR big data analysis • Redesigning IPR processes

This chapter introduces signposts leading to increasing efficiency of IPRM in companies. Although all chapters contain recommendations, they are especially valuable inside this chapter as they are tightly connected to the gaps within the IPR processes. We warmly suggest the chapter to all prac-

© The Author(s) 2018   137
D. Modic, N. Damij, *Towards Intellectual Property Rights Management*, https://doi.org/10.1007/978-3-319-69011-7_7

titioners as well as all students and researchers interested in the practical intricacies of the processes connected to IPRs.

In the first part the human resource dimension is also presented, pointing out the necessary cooperation of various employees for an efficient IPRM. The next layer is the IPR tools—together with the prospects of big data analysis. We then deliberate on what to think about when redesigning the processes and in the end offer the Activity Table.

7.1   THE HR DIMENSION OF IPRM

As with other business processes in the company, the IPR process is also primarily and foremost fully dependant on people. The human resource table (Table 7.1) presents an additional dimension, the human side of IPR processes. Not only does Fig. 7.1 present human resources (and their departments) involved in IPR process on the individual level, but it also reveals if resources work together. It clearly shows that, for example, IP coordinator (IP(R) department) and technology scout (R&D department) are heavily involved in IPR process, whereas the top management CEO and consultant (design department) to a lower degree. It is evident here as well, with IPR process as with other business processes, it is about the people involved.

Note also that the individuals have very different titles, nonetheless we try to give generic titles. The concept of an IP coordinator has not yet been widely embraced, and we see it sometimes under the name of the patent counsel as well. An IP coordinator is the guardian of the intellectual property within the firm. Their activities could be divided in several types: daily (e.g. collect invention report, manage IP budget), additional (document patent usage, use competitor observation tool, participate in or coordinate the observation of competitors' actions, participate in inventors' remuneration, etc.), and mid-term tasks (support IP portfolio management, support IP valuation, involvement in licensing, and IPR-based cooperation contracts). The role of an IP coordinator is to understand what should be done and see that it is done in a timely fashion to allow for the optimal exploitation of IPR by the company. The patent engineer takes on a more technical role: by performing activities such as drafting the specifications and preparing reference figures for patent applications and giving technical expertise during invention evaluation. The emphasis is however on R&D while including patent considerations (not the other way around). Nonetheless, we can also see both types of activities performed by the same person and companies having only one or the

Table 7.1   Activity Table of sub-processes IP creation and IP pre-evaluation

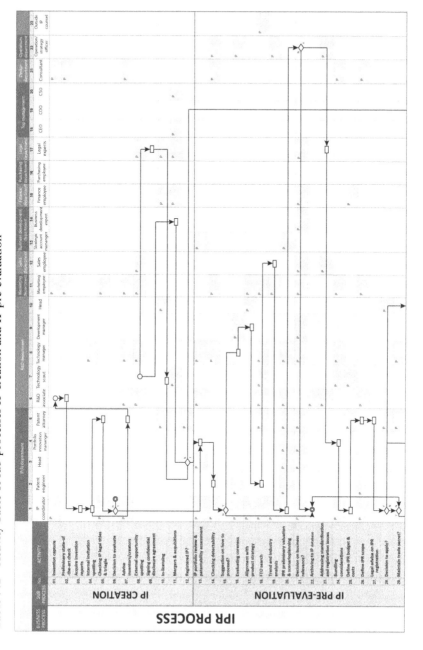

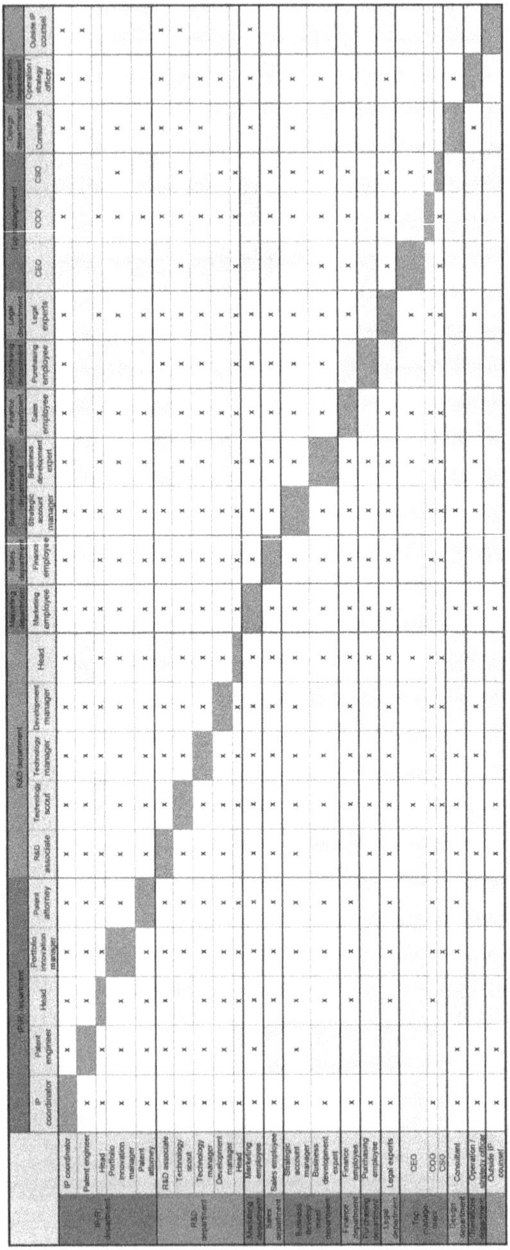

Fig. 7.1 Human resources cross-table

other type of employee—we have, in Table 7.1, divided both into two entities. On the other hand, we did not divide the paralegal and the patent attorney into two separate entities—as their foci are similar and IPR considerations prevail. Nonetheless, a paralegal (though often later pursuing the proper education to become a patent attorney) is the one performing the formal activities behind filings and is also a key employee during the IPR registration as they are often the main contact with all offices. The patent attorney is one of the key employees in all sub-processes.

Next, another role (or in smaller firms a function) that will inevitably become recognized as businesses become more sophisticated in order to operate in the highly competitive world marketplace by exploiting the IPR is the IP portfolio manager. A patent portfolio can be a significant part of a corporation's overall value; thus companies should pay the same level of attention on their patent portfolio as they do on their other investment portfolios. Hence asset allocation, scale, diversification, buy, and hold (the pruning of the portfolio) must all be taken into account. The activities are thus strongly connected also with strategic considerations, and in that regard, the role of the IP portfolio manager is close to that of the head of IP or head of IPR department. The head of the IP department is much more involved in the strategic decisions in regard to the IPR, IPR process optimization, HR decisions, and so on. We have already also mentioned that sometimes there is a single role for different functions, for example, that of IP coordinator, patent engineer, and patent attorney.

We move now to other departments. Inside the R&D department and the business development department, the following employees deserve a mention: R&D associate, technology manager, development manager, the head, the technology scout, strategic account manager, and the business development expert. When speaking with practitioners, there is a great diversity in their job titles. For example, an R&D associate is also called researcher, inventor, engineer, senior investigator, and application scientist, or a technology scout is also called technology scouting manager, open innovation team leader, and global expert for technology access. Employees from other departments are also involved in individual activities: those from marketing department, sales and purchasing, operations and finance department, design department, and the legal department. The latter playing an especially important role as it strongly supports or leads a variety of activities especially inside the commercialization and the enforcement sub-processes. Also the top management involvement is sometimes required within the IPR process as well as needs to be involved in IPR strategy creation (for more on this, consult also Chap. 6).

What we can see there are many individuals that are involved in the IPR process. Furthermore, as the whole process is an interconnection of Back-office, Front-Office, and Mixed activities, we can see that in an ideal case, they would often interact inside different activities.

Often different teams will be formed inside companies, either those dealing with more strategic issues (for this see more also in Chap. 6) or those dealing with the operational level. Strategic patent councils or committees are according to our interviewees comprised usually of Chief Technology Officers/Chief Science Officers (or technology managers) of business units—also sometimes the division CEO—representatives from legal and strategy (or business development) departments and the IPS leadership team (sometimes patent attorneys responsible for a certain segment). For example, in our case of the German conglomerate manufacturing and electronics company, they would meet one year per division or per business unit. Operative patent councils or committees are somewhat more diverse. Usually there is one per business unit, if the company is comprised of several units. The trademark coordinator will usually take the place of the IP coordinator when it is a trademark-related IPR process. Nonetheless, in some cases the trademark coordinator and the head of communications may be involved even if protection is sought for a patent. Also the head of R&D or technology managers are involved. Another key player is the patent attorney (or alternatively for trademarks the trademark attorney). On a daily basis the researchers will often interact with this process. Operative teams make sure that the strategical goals are being operationalized in individual IPR processes.

Keep in mind that in everyday business operation, some will be omitted from the process, either due to a lack of human resources; due to the fact that the same person performs different functions, the type of IPR, the reluctance of people to cooperate, and the mode of protection; or due to the perceived rationality.

For [company] there is a single role for IP coordinator, patent engineer and patent attorney.
Ideally you have the patent attorney, the R&D management and somebody from marketing/sales (the latter most of the time missing) in the patent committee.
Chief IP Counsel,
German International Automotive Supplier

I would say the big advantage was that in our company, the IP department was part of the research department, and unlike many cases, a part of the legal department. Thus regarding the rest of the research department, it was easier to create trust between the people involved. Engineers are not afraid, because they know the staff involved. Often engineers do not like formalised IP processes. They think it is a legal issue and have no interest in them, so there is a reluctance to cooperate. However, the most important step was to make all knowledge available and understandable, thus achieving smoother cooperation.

Ex-Chief Trademark Counsel,
German multinational automotive supplier

Cooperation often goes beyond the IP department. Nonetheless, a reluctance to cooperate due to not understanding the significance of IPR to the business as a whole (i.e. the company) and the benefits for the cooperating department is often present.

An understanding of IPR in sales and purchasing can be problematic. For example what is the advantage for sales? Consider this example. The sales unit would sometimes point out to the customer that this is a patent protected product feature and that our company is the only provider of this. However, the customer might want to have, or even demand to have a possibility of a second source. For customers purchasing organisation this could be a "no-go" for the purchase, then the sales unit could make the pitch that in that case the company is open to licensing to somebody else. Understanding the problem and also ways to resolve it is the key. That also requires training. We could say something similar for purchasing, but vice versa.

Chief IP Counsel,
German international automotive supplier

Let us consider the specific issue of employee remuneration. As it is subjected to legal regulation, this process has to be absolutely formalised with having the interface to the inventions disclosures at the beginning following the process of creating intellectual property right. This might be already somewhat different to what was the original intention and/or scope of the invention. Then we need to have an interface with the marketing and sales department, because the remuneration is calculated as a ratio based on the value of the innovation for the overall business and you need the finance and the sales department to deliver figures. Next, you need to look into the specific status for each IPR and then calculate the remuneration for each inventor. And then comes the issue of the pay cheques. All in all you need at least five departments linked together by just one type of activity.

Ex-Chief Trademark Counsel,
German multinational automotive corporation

Training is often needed due to new hires, the shift of people between departments, or in order to keep the IPR team members (or other employees) on the same awareness level. The top IP executives we inter-viewed focus on three different ways of internal IP department training: learning-by-doing, written protocols, or trainings. The important seg-ments that were put forward are training on procedures and administra-tion, invention spotting, and specific training on patent examination. Hence, companies also aim to generate better IPR results via training. Consider the two examples in Box 7.1.

Box 7.1 Big IPR savvy companies as hubs of IPR training: The case of German manufacturing and electronics company and the European multinational pharmaceutical company

Some of our IPR experts come from companies with several hundred employees dealing with IPR. This mirrors itself not only in their cur-rent IPR structure but also has positive externalities as these people change jobs and go to work for some other companies. This fact can be easily seen from LinkedIn searches—where looking at the history of current mid- or top-level employees, you can see listed among their prior positions also the names of our interviewees' affiliations. Basically, what both have is an elaborate internal education system. For example, starting on the administrative side, the manufacturing and electronics company has a number of apprentices learning the job of a patent administrator or in German Patentanwaltsfachangestellte. But they also educate people on other levels, for example, they educate patent attor-neys "from scratch." Young people coming directly from university are given the training and education to pass the examinations for various qualifying examinations (e.g. German, the USA, China). Some compa-nies also run IPR or patent training programs. Among them is also our example of the European multinational pharmaceutical company, where they run a patent trainee program in the end allowing them to prepare for the European patent attorney qualification and qualifying examination by providing training in paralegal work, patent searches, drafting and prosecution, FTO searches, and so on. This is often done on top of sound basic (technology) education as we can see in this case of a patent counsel from Merck, who points out (Koester 2014): "A sound education in chemistry is essential to identifying and assessing inventions that have the potential for new product development. For example, I receive from our research departments very intricate and chemistry-specific examples to analyse. The challenge is to formulate a concept that covers the specifics in detail but is also broad enough to

cover a larger field." Additional internal training thus gives the employ-ees of the IPR departments' comprehensive IPR training, equipping them to optimize their activities.
Sources:

Koester, V. (2014). Career: A chemist who deals with patents. doi:10.1002/chemv.201400066.

Nonetheless, not to be neglected is training for other employees. For employees in marketing especially there is how to include IPR in marketing pitches; for purchasing there is understanding the benefits of IPRs in order to be able to demand better prices and similar for sales. We already addressed the issue of how good communication between, for example, the sales department and the IP department can help keep trademarks alive (see Chap. 2)—and help achieve IPR strategic goals; but now consider the below case of good cooperation helping enhance the product sales capacities.

You can tell the people in the sales department that this company might come up with a solution to a certain problem, so they need to be prepared. If you have a tender—you have to compete against them, you have to have an answer as to how you can do something better now. That means monitoring what competitors, suppliers, customers are doing in order to learn.

Chief IP Counsel,
German international automotive supplier

The R&D community is another segment where its training is extremely important. The main goal is to raise awareness on IPR. Some specific aims include understanding the purpose and system of IPR; understanding employee obligations and rights in regard to IPR; understanding trade secrets, competition, and FTO analysis; and increasing their skills for invention spotting.

I think the "holy grail" is combining IPR processes with the rest of the business, so people know when to come to you. Otherwise, a number of people in IPR can spend hours and hours in meetings waiting for that golden nugget. It is much more effective, if we train others to see the golden nugget for themselves. This I would call awareness.

Head of Legal Operations and IP Management,
European multinational pharmaceutical company

One of the main foci is hence to get people to come or to communicate with the IPR department early on. Coming late means rushing the IPR activities, thus heightening the potential for making mistakes. This is also related to the importance many IPR executives attach to the early spotting of commercially valuable inventions. The second foci are more related to the freedom to operate perspective: making sure not to begin product development without checking that the IP situation is clear, because that can lead to expensive mistakes. One of the hidden benefits of having people that are focused primarily on IPR issues is that they can neutralize the effect of other people involved (especially in R&D) due to their over attachment in the project they are participating in.

We have identified all human resources involved in the IPRM process, individually as well as from the departmental dimension. When looking at human resources from the process management perspective, we see that, firstly, both structures enable us to identify the required resources to perform all activities transforming the input into the value-added output, and secondly, this provides sufficient data generation to measure potential resource utilization and, consequently, identify resources "stuck" in bottleneck activities. This approach allowed us to not only clearly show the resources working together in the delivery of particular activities but also the base for the Activity Table technique implementation (see Sect. 7.3) that will present the TAD IPR model.

7.2   IPR Automatization, IPR Management Tools, and a Glimpse at Big Data

The next layer is the IPRM tools—as the operationalization of the IPR automatization efforts (going in some parts hand in hand with formalization, as discussed in one of the previous chapters). The IPR management tools are the proverbial shovel; they can either benefit the automatization and formalization or simply play a role of another layer of complexity. Thus it is important—as their role increases—they aim at decreasing or at least managing complexity.

Our respondents have been noticing the growing importance of IT and IT management on IPR management. Some even called it mind-blowing. One of the reasons is due to the fact the more transparent the IPR, the easier is for the company and especially the management to understand its value. Hence, software tools, helping the companies to realize the value from their IP assets, are on the rise. New functions are added all the time.

Often a new provider will pop up, although it seems a certain consolidation is occurring in this service sector.

Some companies use a plethora of different software tools connected to IPR and IPR management. Others try to find software that integrates as many features as possible and also connects to other business processes and databases. Nonetheless, opinions can be heard leading to the belief that sometimes the tools promise more than they deliver, many times (nice visualizations notwithstanding) staying at the level of docketing tools.

Docketing is a well-known activity among the legal professionals. If you ask a lawyer, the traditional answer would be that docketing has to do with deadlines. However, docketing has evolved in two directions: one, docketing now helps do much more than just catch all the necessary deadlines; and two, docketing is a well-known activity (albeit sometimes referred to by some other name) beyond the legal expertise activities (e.g. project management requires a lot of "docketing"). Hence, our next question to IPR executives was are IPR tools comprehensive (Fig. 7.2)?

Fig. 7.2 Are IPR tools comprehensive? Legend: green = positive attribution; red = negative attribution

Fig. 7.3 Home-made (or tailor-made) and commercial IPR tools

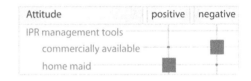

As you can see above, about half of the time our respondents point out positive attributes of the IPR tools they use. Some of them use commercially available tools, other home-made solutions. One of the respondents pointed out that they use a software solution developed by one of their spin-offs. It is when they use home-made solutions that they point out the positive attributes of the tool more often (see Fig. 7.3).

Based on the information presented above, we can see that the more comprehensive the tool, the less information is missing and, consequently, the higher the satisfaction level when the tool is being used. Does this mean that home-made tools that are generally more comprehensive ones are linked to lower error levels when dealing with IPR processes? The indication is that this isn't necessarily so, but it depends on internal skills to develop such a tool or budget restrains (if using home-made solutions or ordering a tailor-made solution) and the willingness of the external provider (for commercially available tools) to adapt the tool to their customers' needs.

However, some errors are directly linked to the use of the tool, as there can be some missing information the tool is simply not using. The missing input that the software tool is not using (and additionally cannot or would not be manually added) can be seen as a disadvantage as it covers the actual gaps—hence also making the need for optimization less easily detectable.

If you are looking for a good/comprehensive IPR tool, what should you look for? What should it be able to do?

I do not think there are any particularly good IP management tools on the market. What I would say is that we have IP docketing tools; we have large databases storing large amount of information—but the primary purpose of that is as support for the Back office administration. What I think the whole industry still lacks are real IP management tools, helping to relate to the business value more.

Head of Legal Operations and IP Management,
European multinational pharmaceutical company

The IPR tool does need to provide a comprehensive docketing system—some of our interviewees call it an administration or documentation system. In this sense it can allow the use of solely electronic files and archive. IPR tools as docketing tools encompass *inter alia*: supplying or channelling invention disclosures to pertinent individuals, providing information regarding communication with the IPR office (deadlines for response to an IPR office action, providing correct forms, notifying about the fees payment deadlines—in other words—providing basic information on IPR maintenance, etc.). Furthermore, what is normally needed, besides giving an overview of own files, is for them to have functions for IT valuation, evaluation, and giving additional opportunities for statistics.

But in larger systems it is also important that it can give orders or shift orders from one IP department to the other IP department—or from the IP department to other departments and vice versa. We will look more closely at some other functions a comprehensive IPR tool should perform, such as data analytics (related to prior art, valuation, commercialization, IPR landscape, etc.), but let us stop at the visualization of data for a second. The visualization is usually connected to evaluation or commercialization information—which is logical if you think about the connection between, for example, IP attorneys and business, when having the opportunity to graphically outline something or to make something simply available that of course is a big step forward, as was put forward by quite a few of our interviewees. Consult also the next citation in order to see that IP experts are interested in IPR tools providing additional visualization.

> *I would say there is definitely a need for optical information, e.g. for drawings of patent information. This would allow the engineers to instantly find out the workings of the invention and not be forced into reading the texts. Because the wording is problematic to understand for a lay person. They need access to the sketches, to the drawings, to easily stroll through them. Because to them a figure is more than a thousand words. They think in figures. In other words, they can more easily discover what the invention is by examining the drawing. The figures are of course available also today, but the way to browse through them should be made more easily accessible. I think it's a problem that often, when we discuss these topics, we take a view from the inside of our IP department. We should go outside and look from there.*
>
> *Ex-Chief Trademark Counsel,*
> *German multinational automotive corporation*

The features mentioned above in the text and citations can help you identify an IPR software that is appropriate for you. At the same time you need to be aware of the fact that this is a process that needs to be done very carefully. You need to keep in mind that changing the software requires a lot of time and resources and even larger and stronger companies struggle with the implementation of a (new) software IPR tool.

> *Integrating your processes into a tool is very costly and time-consuming; the same goes if you decide to change from one tool to another. That's why you tend to stick with the same tool, even if you see optimization potential.*
>
> Chief IP Counsel,
> *German international automotive supplier*

Most of the respondents either have a positive view on the potential of big data on IPR or at least see (mostly still not well defined) potential of such an analysis (see Fig. 7.4). So what should big data analysis be able to bring to the table? We provide an overview in Fig. 7.5.

As mentioned above, we can read quite extensively on different IPR tools. While some of their features are to some extent described, some are not well defined at all, and we are left to wonder what lies beyond. Here we will describe some of the features businesses are looking for (or should be looking for), when deciding on an IPR tool.

We often hear that IPR databases (patent databases and other IP databases) are a wealth of information. This premise also lies in the heart of all IPR systems (together with ensuring distinctiveness in a broad sense); the applicant gains a temporal monopoly in exchange for publicly disclosing certain information and knowledge. Hence, one of the "must" features is that the IPR tools support processes connected to IPR, allowing the access to structured information about the previous state of the art. The general data regarding the validity of these IPRs needs to be included. Connected to IPR data from IPR databases is the related data from publications—harvesting this data from publication databases or general search engines. All of the above put together allows the users of an IPR tool to gain a comprehensive insight into the state of the art—either to build upon it, help the reverse engineering processes, or gain first clues regarding the freedom to operate.

Although we could already label this enriched IPR data, it is still rather crude. Let us point out two issues. *Firstly*, what is the quality of these IPRs? There are several indicators and metrics to approximate the "worth" of IPR through attribution to the quality of IPR.

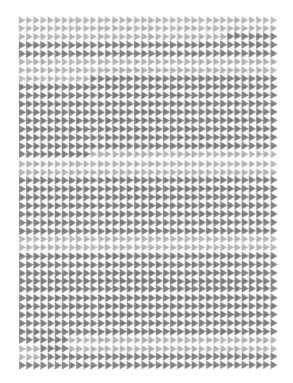

Fig. 7.4 The potential of big data analysis for IPR. Legend: green = positive attribution; red = negative attribution

Secondly, what companies want to know is who the real owner of a certain IPR actually is. The reassignment data is hard to find; in the USA only recently was the reassignment data made available. No real analysis is available as of the time of publication of this monograph, and although some IP executives are aware of them, the experience in utilizing this data is missing according to our interviews. Connected to this is the data about whether the invention is truly being applied; is it implemented in some service, product, or process and by whom?

Some warn that good visualization does not make for a good IPR software tool. We agree. Nonetheless, efforts to visualize the information are appreciated and sought after by IP executives, as it allows both easier communication with business executives (as part of the Front-office) as well as

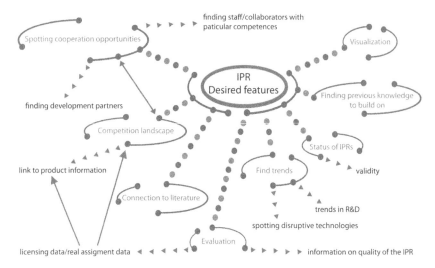

Fig. 7.5 Desired features of IPR tools including big data analysis

providing support to other internal stakeholders—such as researchers (as part of the Back-office). It is important to be able to confer data in a simple and expressive way to allow for business decision to be built upon it; and to be able to present some competitors' research effort or efforts in figures or graphs to researchers, who are usually more prone to think in visualizations than words.

What are the problems of big data analysis in practice today? What is it that worries IP experts who work for IP savvy multinational companies? There are five types of major problems with big data analysis:

Firstly. There is a lack of data—for those attempting to deliver solutions from outside the company, there is a lack of internal data, thwarting their ability to validate their models. For those attempting to find solutions inside the companies, the lack of external data is sometimes the biggest problem (e.g. data about who is the real owner of a certain IPR). The solution that would enable the scientists to develop new methods and tools seems to be in cooperation between scientists from inside and outside the company.

Secondly. Although some indicators are robust, they are designed in a way that IP experts from business are sometimes not prepared to acknowledge their validity—as they are convinced the indicators may have some merit on a generalized level, but their business usefulness is lacking. An indication of patent quality on the basis of the length of patent claims is a good example of that opinion.

Thirdly. The problem of methods breaking down on smaller datasets seems to be one of the crucial problems of big data analysis at the moment. This means that although big data analysis has potential, can it be said that it is useful for smaller companies?

Fourthly. Most of the big data analysis which is used uses historical data. However, the companies are interested in the future, not so much the past—also in terms of IPR. Hence, simulation techniques, data bursting techniques, and other similar methods will probably need to come to the forefront, together with making sure all methods and results are truly robust.

Lastly. A consideration must be given to twofold models. Clearly, there is enormous wealth of IPR big data—nonetheless it seems a certain human deliberation cannot be skipped at the end. This also means that emphasis should be given to clear, simple, and understandable interfaces and visualizations of data.

> *I am always happy that people do analyses—as long as they understand the limitations of their analysis that's all fine. It is people attributing more value to what they are doing than is actually the case...Then it is all good if it is within the limitations of the method and the conclusions you are able to reach.*
> *Head of Legal Operations and IP Management,*
> *European multinational pharmaceutical company*

In this chapter we explore the IPR tools, not so much *as-is*, but mostly what their potential can be. We try to emphasize that they should be more than docketing tools. Furthermore, we take a look at the potential of big data for IPR analysis and point out at some limitations. We also warn of the lock-in when a certain tool is used, although as we will point out in the next subchapter that, on the other hand, when changing the IPR tool, it might be a good time to rethink and potentially redesign some parts of the IPR process.

7.3   What Should You Worry About When Designing or Re-modelling Your IPR Processes?

IPR process design or re-modelling is a never-ending task—as long as a company is actively participating in IPR protection (in any form), so long its focus needs to be put on how efficient their processes are; what was the efficient IPR process yesterday is probably already a less efficient process today and definitely will be the inefficient process of tomorrow. There is always a lot of thought given to re-modelling or optimizing the IPR processes themselves. This can be done by internal pushes or internal pulls.

> *We have practice teams. I lead the IP services team. We share information, people go to conferences, they talk to other companies, they talk amongst themselves etc. Our basic idea is; we funnel suggestions—sometimes triggered by internal learning, sometimes triggered by external forces—and we use that to develop further our processes. I think we are actually pretty good doing that. The same goes for our attorneys. The attorneys have a practice team and review processes regarding patents and develop new guidelines or internal solutions. Since our company is a large one, it is possible to set aside some time for a number of individuals to fulfil these functions—which is a difficult in a small group.*
>
> Head of Legal Operations and IP Management,
> European multinational pharmaceutical company

One of our IPR experts pointed out that anytime you change something you can start rethinking what you can change in your setup, so that the things will run more smoothly. Keep in mind that an IP manager can also positively use the change of a software tool in order to optimize IPR processes. A successful integration of a new tool demands careful assessment of IPR processes in order to evaluate what kind of a tool the company really needs. Furthermore, seeing the features the software brings might be a good opportunity to think about further options to improve parts where bottlenecks occur and think of additional activities which might bring value to the internal or external stakeholder or the business. Keep in mind that our IPR experts emphasized that reviewing the process periodically is extremely helpful and leads to improved IPR practices. This goes for both adding layers (such as opting to conduct additional analysis, include more data, include another employee in a certain activity) and taking away layers that have been seen as not necessary. For example, one of our interviewees is involved in a process that has two main goals: one is harmonization and the other is simplification. Inside the company, a systematic audit is performed with a focus on simplifying.

Let us now focus on what parts of the IPR process the interviewed IPR experts see as especially critical: the early harvesting and clearing process (as the most important ones) as well as the decision to file an IPR right and the process of evaluating the IPR.

Early harvesting needs to be supported firstly with strong cooperation between researcher, developers, and the IPR experts (or in other words good developed HR dimension) and secondly with an information system that allows the transfer of accurate IP data in a speedy, structured, and coherent manner (or developed infrastructure dimension). This needs to then be backed also by support for further steps and good feedback information. Knowledge management inside these early on activities is of key importance.

Clearing process is also essential as it prevents the unnecessary spending of time, money, and other resources for inventions that do not have a future in the real world, or in other words where the freedom to operate relying on the invention in question and the connected right to appropriate the derived value from it are put to question.

> *The /.../critical part is the so-called Clearing process step, so the given product is ready to be on the market, i.e. that we have done all the clearances in order to make sure that we are not running into problems with others IP rights, that could have been foreseen. /.../If you have not done the mandatory clearing of the products before you put them on the market, then the likelihood that you run into problems for certain parts of IP rights is much higher than if you had done such a clearing process at the certain time before the product is put on the market.*
>
> *Chief IP Counsel,*
> *German Conglomerate manufacturing and electronics company*

The decision whether to file a patent or not is one of the essential decisions of the IPR processes. If decided against, the plethora of non-formal protection mechanisms are still available (e.g. keeping something as a trade secret, publishing the results as to prevent others from patenting a certain invention, or registering a certain design, and so on, or to simply energize a certain evolving field) as the alternative to doing nothing. Some other critical points are also mentioned sometimes: those connected to the evaluation of the IPR, uncertainties that are arising from the IPR system itself, the problems connected with three decision points (or so-called gateway activities): the decision to demand a higher margin, the decision to enforce the IPR, and the decision to abandon the IPR. This also brings us again to the importance of the alignment with the commercial and product strategy of the company (which is as we have mentioned before the common point with innovation and IP management—IPR management however in certain cases manages to disambiguate itself from the product development process to a certain point, when recognizing value in IPR in itself—otherwise the integration and interplay with the product lifecycle management is of key importance and is realized through multiple common formalized decision points).

There are two critical elements our respondents point out time and again: time and (human) error. Almost 12% of all coded segments are related to time considerations. Getting input to the involved internal and external stakeholders (which is connected to quality management of internal relationships and efficient communication) and reacting on time thus realizing maximum business value. This also again brings us to smooth processes framed by efficiency and risk management. The latter is also related to error. Errors can stem from poor data quality in itself, poor software tool design, or human errors (mostly connected to a lack of knowledgeability on certain IPR-related issues or a lack of harmonized process). The above-mentioned gateway processes (the decision to enforce a patent and the decision to ask for a higher margin) can be particularly affected by errors—mistakes in all three of them easily result in diminished returns, additional costs, or the inability to further harvest the benefits of IPRs.

To conclude, when thinking what part of the processes should be especially nurtured, the IP executives pointed out the following strong points of their own processes—where considerable efforts have been made to improve those parts: (1) Raising awareness internally. (2) Having strong stage-gate processes—which also includes deliberation on the necessity of specific mechanisms such as second attorney oversight and carefully thought through notification of abandonment system. The latter is important in smaller companies as these often have problems identifying the (additional) potential of their IPRs and in larger companies as their activities can be very diverse and the centralized unit may not have sufficient oversight in terms of the necessity and all uses of a certain IPR. (3) Implementing past experience—although extremely important, this issue is sometimes on the back track. Even some multinationals struggle with implementing systems for efficient feedback and the analysis of this feedback. (4) Developing defensive mechanisms—ex ante development of activities and processes connected to defending your IPR in the business world. This also represents some signposts where to begin, would a company try to redesign their IPR process.

7.4   Using TAD IPR and the Answers to IPR Process Redesign/Optimization It Can Bring

This section focuses on the presentation of the TAD IPR model by using the Activity Table approach. Due to its size and complexity, the model is split into several tables. As presented in detail in Chap. 3, the aim of this approach is to present the generic model of the IPRM process with identified activities on one hand and identified human resources on the other. This is achieved by connecting every activity horizontally to a resource or team of resources (presented in columns) participating in the execution of each activity. As seen in Tables 7.1, 7.2, and 7.3, the majority of identified

Table 7.2   Activity Table of sub-processes IP registration and IP commercialization

Table 7.3 Activity Table of sub-processes infringement and IP post-evaluation

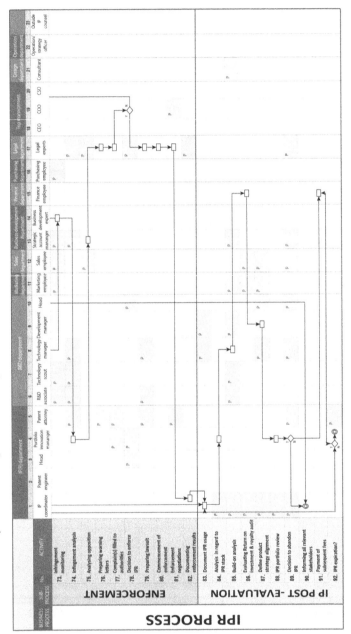

activities are linked to a number of resources (at least one). The cell in the crossroad between the resource, responsible or accountable for the execution of a specific activity (defined in the column), and the activity itself (defined in the row) contains any of the following symbols □, ◊, ○, or ⊙. Each of these symbols illustrated a different state of the activity: □ demonstrates an activity without any condition regarding its execution, ◊ demonstrates an activity where a decision (either Yes (Y) or No (N)) needs to be made in order to proceed, ○ demonstrates a start activity that only produces an output, whereas ⊙ demonstrates the end activity. The letter P on the row of each activity shows the team members also included in the execution of that activity. The vertical linkage, on the other hand, is used to define the order of the execution of the activities by linking every activity with its predecessor and successor activity/ies.

The IPR process model presented in Table 7.1 shows the first two (out of the six) sub-processes—IP creation and IP pre-evaluation. Also, it shows all human resources participating in the process, grouped together by the department they belong to. We have identified 11 departments and additional outside IP counsel. From the model, it is clearly seen that the majority of activities in both sub-processes are performed in either the IP(R) department or the R&D department with participating resources also from sales, business development, legal, and operations departments.

The symbol ○ in cell(1,6) shows the start of the IPR process (one of the two starts). The other start is shown in cell(8,7). Based on the success of the preliminary activities, the IPR process can be finished early in the IP creation sub-process should the decision to evaluate be negative, or in the IP pre-evaluation sub-process should the decision on business relevance also be negative and result in archiving to IP database.

The symbol □ in cell(2,6) in the IP creation sub-process illustrates that the activity preliminary state-of-the-art check is carried out by an R&D associate with the help of the marketing employee and the consultant from the design department. Furthermore, the symbol ◊ in cell(12,3) means that the activity 12—registered IP—is a decision activity, carried out by resource 3—the head of the IP(R) department with the consult from the patent attorney. Such an activity starts different alternative paths and is succeeded by a different alternative—if IP is registered, the IPR process continues in the IP commercialization sub-process (see Table 7.2) by performing the decision to actively use activity. If, however, IP is not registered, the IPR process continues in the IP pre-evaluation sub-process by the portfolio innovation manager reviewing the IP portfolio and patentability assessment with the help of the IP coordinator, the head of the IP(R) department and the R&D associate, the technology manager (both from R&D department), and the strategic account manager. Cell(14,2) shows that the patent engineer checks detectability with the assistance of the IP portfolio manager, the technology manager, marketing employee, operation/strategy officer, and consultant from the design department. All but the first three are employed in the Front-office department but are nonetheless also strongly involved the Back-office or Mixed activities. Checking detectability is important as it decides on protecting mechanisms (whether to use the formal or informal ones) on one hand and valuing as well as rating inventions on the other.

As such, it strongly influences the decision process and is sometimes built on the use of various qualitative-based scales. An example of such is shown below[1]:

1. Without specific know-how or background knowledge on the particulars of the implementation, the invention is undetectable.
2. The invention is detectable via experimentation by experts in the field.
3. The invention is detectable through a targeted investigation and experimentation or by complex re-engineering.
4. The invention is detectable through inspection and observation and/or via simple re-engineering practices.
5. Detectable through casual inspection/competitor advertising.

Another important activity is in cell(16,8) named evaluating coreness. It is performed by the technology manager from the R&D department with also participating IP coordinator, and patent engineer from the IP(R) department, development manager from the R&D department, and operation/strategy officer from the operations department. The reason that so many resources are included in this activity lies in the potential consequences of their decision as it presents an informed overview on whether or not the invention is relevant or obsolete or irrelevant. Firstly, if the decision is that the invention is relevant or core then the output (the invention report) will cover future patents that will be central to company's current and future operation, providing exclusivity with respect to product/process, providing necessary FTO. They are a key part of a strategically planned patent fence or maintain exclusive franchise/monopoly they were intended to secure (will be used as key strategic patents).

Secondly, if the decision is that the invention is obsolete or non-core, then the invention report will cover technologies that are useful or potentially useful, but they are not critical to the companies' competitive position, for example, inventions that would be easy to "design around" even if patented, those promising a financial gain on IPR markets and not the goods markets (e.g. via licensing, IPR title transfers, etc.) or also (more applicable later on) inventions related to products that were decided not to be on market. Finally, if the decision is that the invention is irrelevant or useless, then the invention report needs to focus on covering obsolete technologies, technological dead ends (more often applicable further on), or inventions conferring no competitive advantage and offer no reasonable likelihood of generating revenues.

Focusing on the IP pre-evaluation sub-processes, there are three consecutive activities in cell(18,2) FTO search, cell(19,12) trend and industry analysis, and cell(20,1) IPR preliminary valuation and scenario planning that are a part of IPR risk management. The first and the latter are executed in the IP(R) department; the middle one is executed in the sales department. By focusing on the last out of the three, the IPR preliminary valuation can be twofold dependant on what stage of the process is being done. In the early stages, the valuation would be based by comparing the invention under valuation to other IPs, whereas in the later stages the metrics with various factors would be used, for example, analysing similar deals on the market or looking at the raw economic value of the invention.

Table 7.2 presents the continuation of the IPR process model; particularly it presents the third and fourth sub-process named IP registration and IPR commercialization. As with the previous two sub-processes, all involved resources are grouped by departments. The model clearly shows that activities in the IP registration sub-process are executed by resources in the IPR department, particularly by the portfolio innovation manager and patent engineer with assistance from other resources in the department as well as resources from the R&D marketing, sales, business development, finance, and legal departments. Hence, it is clearly seen from the model that that activities in the IP registration are either BO activities or Mixed activities.

The model also identifies a number of loops, linked to the conditional activities (where decisions on how to proceed, if at all, need to be made); for example, the symbol ◊ in cell(40,5) shows that a decision needs to be made whether or not to drop the IPR application. Should the company decide to continue with the IPR application, the amended application is sent in (cell(42,5)), and based on the IPR office feedback (cell(43,5)), the decision to drop the IPR application is made again (cell(40,5)).

On the other hand, in the IPR commercialization sub-process, the majority of activities are executed in the departments that carry out the FO or Mixed activities and only eight activities in the BO. As the aim of the IPR commercialization sub-process deals with IPR coming to market, this is not a surprise. Though focusing on the IPR success after the IPR is registered, the (generic) model shows that this is a less complex set of activities as the sub-process prior with only one loop (cell(63,13), cell(64,13), and cell (65,13)) and two stage-gate activities (cell(54,19) and cell(59,14)).

Table 7.3 presents the last two sub-processes of the IPR process model, named enforcement and IPR post-evaluation. The structure of the table is again the same as in previous two models, having activities grouped by the sub-processes and resources by departments. The majority of enforcement activities are executed in the Front-office departments; particularly they are carried out in the legal department by the legal expert with the help of an innovation portfolio manager and/or a patent attorney; for example, the cell(77,14) shows that the activity complain(s) filed to authorities is performed by the legal expert with the participation of both the innovation portfolio manager and patent attorney (both marked with a letter P). Even though no loops are present in this model, the sub-process is still complex as it influences the cash flow of the company.

The final sub-process that concludes the IPR business process is the IPR post-evaluation sub-process. Here, the majority of activities are performed in the Back-office departments with mainly the help from either the sales, marketing, or business development department. The two Front-office activities are executed by the finance employee from the finance department, for example, cell(90,15) and cell(95,15). This sub-process is additionally important as it evaluates all IPRs again, comparing them to their initial valuations as some IPRs that were initially valuated as high value added later materialize in a lesser or even non-value adding at all.

Symbol ⊙ in cell(i,j) shows that the activity i is the final/end activity of a particular process flow and is executed by the activity j; for example, cell(90,1) informing all relevant stakeholders is the final activity within that process flow, and as its output, it produces a note to stakeholders regarding the specific IPR. The IP coordinator informs all relevant stakeholders, especially all departments utilizing the abandoning IPR and the inventor. Generally, an end activity has two focuses. The first one deals with ensuring that the proper protocols to archive the invention (with, if possible, easy recall options) are set, and the second one is oversight and implemented control as to not abandon it without sufficient insights on its utility gathered.

> *We have a number of mechanisms in place for second attorney reviews. I think that is important. Oversight. I will give you two examples of oversight. When we draft patent applications, we have a second attorney review it. Also, prior to abandonment of the IPR, we have a process for ensuring that other parts of the business are notified in order to make sure that it is not of interest to them.*
> *Head of Legal Operations and IP Management,*
> *European multinational pharmaceutical company*

Analysing/presenting IPR process with the use of Activity Table provides us with the following: (1) in graphical form and with the use of easily understandable symbols, the table presents an IPR process model in a transparent mode; (2) it clearly shows the more/less utilized human resources within the IPR process, thus enabling modifications in reallocating or adding additional resources to the process; (3) it establishes the relationships/connections between all activities within the process, thus identifying loops and any potential challenges the company could face when redesigning the IPR process. The IPR process model presented in the Activity Table is in fact an IPR process "blueprint" and as such also a starting point for any additional analyses such as process simulation or network analyses. We believe it to be more specific than most usually presented processes, allowing also to check which of the activities are performed and which are perhaps missing now (either as an individual activity or as a part of an activity), thus allowing to detect the gaps.

The aim of this chapter was to investigate the IPRM in practice by focusing on three key perspectives. Firstly, we examined the HR perspective—who is participating in the IRPM process, in what capacity, what department are they from, and most importantly, how and if particular resources work together to perform specific activities. Secondly, the chapter looks closely at IPR automatization and IPRM tools by focusing on their practical side as well as establishing a link between the IPRM and big data. Finally, we provide you with a generic TAD IPR model that describes the IPR process activity by activity, connects resources (and departments) to these activities, introduces their order and the links, as well as clearly presents any identified loops.

NOTES

1. Krajec, R. (2017). Detectability is a key factor for patent valuation. Available at: http://www.blueironip.com/detectability-key-factor-patent-valuation/

CHAPTER 8

Conclusion

Abstract This chapter presents the conclusion of the research emphasizing the main conclusions and presenting directions on how to untangle the intangibles and thereby optimize IPR processes.

Keywords Optimizing IPR process • IPR management • Intangibles

As some of our interviewees emphasized, IPR management (IPRM) is like building a bridge between business and the world of IPR. This monograph is a part of the cohort of works dealing with innovation management (including knowledge management), however focusing strongly on intellectual property rights. On the other hand, it is a part of the literature on IPR—but again with a bit of a twist, as we focus primarily on the processes connected to them and the management of IPR and not on, for example, legal issues. In this way we tried to fill a niche in the literature— the closest literature being that of strategic handling of IPR (e.g. Harrison and Sullivan 2012; Rimai 2016; Thoma 2017).

The monograph thus highlights gaps in efficient IPR management (IPRM) by offering insights into practices used by some top IP experts. It provides a conceptual framework and constructs for IPRM, derived from practical and enriched by theoretical insight. It also brings an IPR process

D. Modic, N. Damij, *Towards Intellectual Property Rights Management*, https://doi.org/10.1007/978-3-319-69011-7_8

optimization model (using the Activity Table approach) to allow us to focus on IPR process, individual sub-processes and activities—together with the connections between them (the flow as well as the cooperation on the level of human resources). Also provided are excerpts from interviews, organizational and managerial recommendations, and short case studies or case-in-points. The latter are very diverse, from some insight into checking detectability at a German multinational industrial conglomerate to showing big IPR savvy companies as hubs for IPR training (in the case of a German manufacturing and electronics company and the European multinational pharmaceutical company). Citations not only provide insights into IPR experts' opinions but also sometimes provide insights into commonly used practices (e.g. that of the internal IPR classification ranking).

As we emphasized in the beginning, IPRM is not an easy task. It is complicated for both small and big companies—from IP Rookies to IPR savvy companies. What we tried to offer here is a guide that will facilitate your journey through the jungle known as IPR. Let us try to sum up some major points expressed inside this monograph in order to achieve the below listed aims.

The monograph focuses on the delivery of the following aims:

1. Offering coherent constructs and conceptual frameworks for IPR management by defining IPR management as a *sui generis* subfield of business process management by:

   (a) Strengthening the theoretical basis of IPR management research
   (b) Defining Back-office and Front-office IPR processes and their connections

2. Highlighting practices of efficient IPR management including state-of-the-art feedback from conducting interviews with IP(R) executives thereby:

   (a) Investigating the difference between IP and IPR process and defining IPRM as a business process from the executives' perspective
   (b) Presenting IPR process flows by creating a generic IPRM process model
   (c) Identifying knowledge (and other) gaps preventing efficient IPR management and presenting solutions to identified gaps

3. Offering an evaluation of existing IPR management models and tools for IPR process modelling giving:

   (a) An in-depth analysis of a TAD methodology-based IPR modelling tool highlighting critical problems in IPR processes

We look into the difference between IPRs and other intangibles. At the beginning of the monograph, we point out the differences in theory (with, e.g. distinctions relating to geographic and temporal scope), however we later focus on the differences in practice (especially the manageability and enforceability). We also offer a brief overview of formal and informal IP protection mechanisms, where we also try to compare them in light of the business processes surrounding them (e.g. in the short case-in-point, we try to delve into issues not usually at the forefront of our thinking—e.g. knowing that it was Kawasaki, who first developed, marketed, and registered the trademark of Jet Ski; the retention of trademarks is thus very important for individual companies and their ability to exploit the IPR, but not at the forefront of deliberations about trademarks by the general public—we point out several cases where this is the case).

The IPR process is introduced as in the interplay of Back- and Front-office activities, which the IPR processes comprise of. We offer a more detailed look into the taxonomy of IPR-related activities to Back- and Front-office activities. Back-office activities are defined as administrative and legal activities—often strongly influenced by external pressures/influences/demands which by themselves do not add value to the IPR. The Front-office activities are designed to enable the maximization of IPR's added value. They are highly dependent on the cooperation between different departments (especially with top management) and external stakeholders. Some activities are so-called Mixed activities, requiring both legal-administrative tasks and business considerations to be employed. The IPR process is hence a sequence of Back-office and Front-office activities, producing end and intermediate results for stakeholders, through which companies or individuals maintain and exploit their patents, designs, trademarks, copyrights, and trade secrets in order to accomplish a variety of defined IPR-related goals, as well as to produce outputs for other processes in the company.

We look at the IPRM processes as business processes from the theoretical as well as the practical point by defining their inputs, value-added outputs, activity sequencing, description, and type to link each activity to either being executed in the Front-office or Back-office department, as well as resource allocation. Case study from Huawei company is presented to further demonstrate the value of IPRM processes being viewed as one of a firm's business processes.

Looking at IPR management, there are two different levels or dimensions we need to pay attention to. First is the IPR process on the level of individual IPR (we talk about them more from a practical point of view especially in Chap. 6 and the end part of Chap. 7). Secondly, there is the strategic level—building a framework for handling IPR (we also dedicate a section on this in Chap. 6 with the emphasis by our interviewees). We emphasize that it is important to thoroughly understand the IPR process, its flow, and activities to successfully employ any of IPR-related strategies and reach IPR-related goals; nonetheless, a change in the strategic goals can cause changes in IPR process, as they need to adapt. All of this furthers our notion that the intellectual property protection processes need to be systematic, carefully designed, and thoroughly thought through.

In order to really understand all aspects of IPRM processes as business processes, collecting real-world data from "live" IPRM processes was crucial. As such, we believe the methodological background is important; we use one of the chapters to introduce the empirical part of the research through a short methodological review demonstrating pertinent experts and the framework of the research protocol and to identify challenges faced. In the chapters dealing with the empirical part of the research, we delve inter alia into the following issues: (a) IPRM not or is the same as IPM, (b) questioning whether formalization is really necessary and if it has the potential to lead to optimization of processes, (c) presenting the attributes of IPRM (integrated, seamless, comprehensive, and outward looking) and functions (information function, etc.). We delve behind attributes such as "integrated" and "aligned" to discern what these mean in practice inside IPR savvy companies. We concern ourselves thus with what is behind these often used monikers. These elements are looked into more deeply also with the aim to define IPR management as a *sui generis* subfield of business process management.

We also take an in-depth look as to what differentiates IPR management from IP management. Historically, IP management as a term is used with the execution of all activities linked with intellectual property rights and was often handled by the R&D departments/people within the IP departments; for example, IBM in 1926 established the patent department that dealt with all aspects of IPR protection. In recent decades however, though the distinction emerged, dealing with IPR would become oftentimes primarily the responsibility of the legal department (even today companies have their IP departments as parts of the legal department—we also offer several organizational models based on conducted interviews). Looking not only from the organizational perspective, IP experts from IPR savvy companies mostly see their work as managing IPR and, to a lesser degree, other non-formalized forms of IP. The scope also seems to be different. The foci of IPRM are IPR and their management. Hence, defining and utilizing IPR assets stands at the forefront of IPRM activities. This goes for both creating them and their commercialization. The key focus here however does not lay with the size of distinction between the two but much more important that both IPRM and IPM need to be aligned with the overall commercial strategy of the company.

In order to evaluate processes as either core or auxiliary, we first looked at the level of process formalization and whether or not it is linked to the process optimization. IPRM process is an especially strongly formalized process. Looking from the process management perspective, process formalization brings process automatization, and once the company reaches this level, they can start considering process optimization by either removing or reducing the identified inefficiencies. Not surprisingly, due to the type of respondents, the prevailing attitude is that of agreeing with the premise of formalization bringing opportunities for optimization. We briefly show what top IP executives have in mind when saying so.

When trying to identify IPRM processes as business processes, we also evaluated IPRM processes in light of either being core or auxiliary processes. IP experts think that IPRM processes are auxiliary if (a) the companies' main focus is product development and IPRs are just a stone in the mosaic; (b) they do not have a goal on its own; (c) they are highly formalized; and (d) their focus is not income generation. However, IPRM processes, as core processes, have all the elements a business process should have—they only start once the input has been identified, they consist of a set of linked parallel and/or consecutive activities (sometimes grouped in either work processes or sub-processes), their end results in an output that has value for the customer. So, does it really matter whether an IPRM process is core or auxiliary? IPR processes are business processes, consisting of an input, linked activities, and producing an output. The quicker the companies recognize IPR processes as business processes, the quicker they could manage them efficiently, thus ensuring the delivery of a high added value output.

Furthermore, to identify IPRM processes as business processes, we investigated the IP experts' point of view, starting with the added value of IPRs and the value IPRM outputs to add to the company. The generic IPRM business process model is presented with the use of the TAD methodology's Activity Table technique as the interpretative framework describing the IPR management practices more in depth. Once the IPRM process was identified as a business process, we used two graphical modelling tools to present it, firstly in flowchart form and secondly in tabular form. The type of activities identified in the IPRM process was also identified, thus showing the balanced process where each activity type was more or less equally presented. The Activity Table tool was used in addition to the vastly used flowchart tool as it contains much more vital information about the process; it not only identifies the activities, their links, and sub-processes (as the flowchart does) but also encompasses activities' inputs, outputs, type, and description. It also connects the activity with the human resources either/both responsible for the execution or participating in the execution of the activity. Inside the monograph, we present a very detailed IPRM process model (on the individual level) consisting of IP creation, IP pre-evaluation, IP registration, IPR commercialization, enforcement, and IPR post-evaluation sub-processes, with the level of detail usually not seen elsewhere (the closest are some models offering an insight solely on IPR registration)—including not even seen in the internal documentation of IPR savvy companies. Below, we show, however, how the emphasis on who are involved within IPR process is not as limited as some models showing or describing solely the IPR registration would lead us to believe. However, we can see that the bulk of responsibility for the third sub-process IPR registration indeed lies with IPR staff, and their involvement is felt overall; nonetheless other sub-processes are much more diverse in terms of human resource involvement. This points out to the importance of good communication and collaboration between involved individuals.

The individual IPR process presented mirrors that of IPR processes in larger companies. It is of course an idealized process, where not all activities will be performed individually and not all employees listed will be involved (as some can be seen as functions in that case). Nonetheless, there are important lessons smaller companies can learn from knowledge about the IPR activity flow within their larger competitors because of the following points. Firstly, using external service providers such as patent attorneys or companies conducting clearance searches on a number of activities (however not all of them) can offer some advantages, yet also some significant disadvantages. Inefficiencies that arise when using external counsel stem from a lack of knowledge about the process, the inability to define the optimal scope of assistance needed as well as optimal timing for acquiring these external services (consider here the issue of timing the clearing activity—if done too early, it may cause issues later—whether due to the need to repeat it or from an unforeseen competitors' reaction). Understanding the IPR process, its activities, their (inter-)connectedness, and processes surrounding them is key to optimizing value extracted from external IPR services—knowledge that we wish to provide. Secondly, smaller companies may benchmark and compare their IPR process in order to use it either as a signpost for their redesign of processes or simply to optimize their individual activities. Hence, our "Robin Hood" approach, involving learning from the big companies to offer to smaller companies, also shows the beauty of intangible assets as through their use and knowledge sharing, nobody is weakened as a consequence (see Fig. 8.1).

As a backdrop to IPRM, as well as to present some possible gaps, three specific perspectives are presented: the human resource perspective, the IPR tools in connection to formalization (including the prospects of IPR big data analysis), and some critical points of IPR processes. IP executives pointed out the following critical points of their own processes and in IPRM:

1. Raising awareness internally and implementing past experience—although extremely important, this issue is sometimes on the back track. Even some multinationals struggle with implementing systems for efficient feedback and analysis of this feedback.
2. Having strong stage-gate processes—which also includes deliberation on the necessity of specific mechanisms such as second attorney oversight and carefully thought through notification of abandonment system.
3. Developing defensive mechanisms—ex ante development of activities and processes connected to defending your IPR in the business world.
4. Inside individual IPR process: early harvesting, clearing process, filing, and abandonment.

However, the top IP executives are not only able to identify the critical points and gaps, they know how to recognize value in different segments; they take a holistic view, where value for the company is seen both in

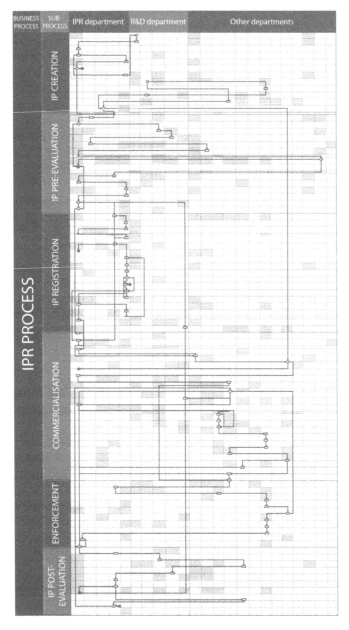

Fig. 8.1 Overall IPR process flow

external value and the value extracted from their providing support to internal stakeholders through various interim outputs. The latter is not to be considered negligible as it strengthens the intellectual property itself and enables the information function of the IPR management.

Redesigning the process (as a whole as well as the critical points described above) is not an easy task and according to our interviewees can be caused by numerous external and internal pushes (e.g. some of our IPR experts have used the change of the IPR tool to thoroughly examine their own processes). To do them well, a good understanding of the current IPR process, its flow, and the involved employees is of key importance as well as the understanding of the options (i.e. knowing the idealized process flow). We hope that this monograph helps to clarify some points as we tried to untangle the intangibles.

REFERENCES

Harrison, S. S., & Sullivan, P. H. (2012). *Edison in the boardroom revisited: How leading companies realize value from their intellectual property: Revisited.* Hoboken, NJ: Wiley.

Rimai, D. S. (2016). *Patent engineering: A guide to building a valuable patent portfolio and controlling the marketplace.* Hoboken, NJ: Scrivener Publishing and Wiley.

Thoma, G. (2017). *Patent management and valuation: The strategic and geographical dimension.* New York: Routledge.

Index[1]

A

Activity, v, 2–6, 11–14, 18, 19, 27, 29, 29n2, 37, 40–44, 46–50, 54, 56, 57, 62, 64–68, 71–74, 76, 78, 79, 85, 87, 89, 90, 92–96, 98, 100, 101, 106, 107, 113, 118, 120, 126, 133, 134, 138, 141, 142, 146, 147, 154–157, 159–164, 166–171

Activity loop, 107, 113, 162

Activity table, 7, 46–49, 98, 101, 133, 138, 139, 146, 157, 158, 163, 170

Aligned, 3, 7, 8, 13, 19, 25, 27, 29, 36, 68, 78, 81, 82, 87, 168, 169

Asset, 3, 14n1, 19, 34, 39–42, 72, 120, 126, 141, 146

Auxiliary, 9, 43, 69, 74, 77–79, 84, 91, 94, 138, 148, 150, 152, 155, 173
  process, 43

B

Back-office, v, 4, 5, 9, 11, 13, 26–28, 29n2, 54, 80, 94, 95, 98, 100, 107, 113, 133, 142, 148, 162, 166–168

Big data analysis, 8, 56, 138, 150–153, 163, 171

Business model, 43–46

Business process, v, xi, 4, 5, 7, 9, 12, 40, 42–44, 46–49, 60, 65, 77, 79, 162, 166, 168–170
  management, xi, 4, 5, 7, 9, 12, 41, 77, 166, 168
  modelling, 43, 44, 46, 50

C

Commercialization subprocess, 92, 96, 120

Communication, 56, 68, 72, 84, 113, 126, 145, 149, 151, 156, 170

---

[1] Note: Page numbers followed by 'n' refers to notes.

© The Author(s) 2018
D. Modic, N. Damij, *Towards Intellectual Property Rights Management*, https://doi.org/10.1007/978-3-319-69011-7

GPSR Compliance
The European Union's (EU) General Product Safety Regulation (GPSR) is a set
of rules that requires consumer products to be safe and our obligations to
ensure this.

If you have any concerns about our products, you can contact us on

ProductSafety@springernature.com

In case Publisher is established outside the EU, the EU authorized
representative is:

Springer Nature Customer Service Center GmbH
Europaplatz 3
69115 Heidelberg, Germany

www.ingramcontent.com/pod-product-compliance
Lightning Source LLC
Chambersburg PA
CBHW070946050326
40689CB00014B/3360